Cracked Open

A Conscious Journey Within

Maria de Los Angeles Urquia

About the Author

Maria de Los Angeles, originally from Honduras, encountered a significant life change at the tender age of 7.5 when she faced separation from her familiar surroundings. Relocating to New York, she found solace with her uncle and his family, where she navigated through numerous challenges and endured traumatic events.

Her path to healing initiated a spiritual transformation, profoundly altering her perspective and approach to life. Currently calling Vancouver, B.C., her home, Maria lives with her supportive family. Possessing a Bachelor of Science in Nursing, she serves as a registered nurse in the downtown east side of Vancouver—a community grappling with various health complexities, including trauma, mental health challenges, and substance use disorders.

In her role, Maria compassionately tends to patients, contributing to the well-being of one of Canada's most vulnerable communities. Beyond her professional commitments, Maria finds joy in dancing, hiking, connecting with nature, practicing yoga and meditation, and exploring different corners of the world. Her deep-seated desire to enhance her spiritual gifts and unravel the mysteries of the universe propels her on an ongoing journey of self-discovery and growth.

A Heartfelt Note

To my brothers and sisters,

Brothers and sisters, I see you. I see how tired you are from all those internal battles you fight in silence. Brothers and sisters, I feel your pain, as I am you, and you are me. I see how you attempt to cover up that void you feel inside. Sisters and brothers, your existence does not need validation or qualifications. It simply is. I want you to know that there is absolutely nothing wrong with you. That you are enough. You are whole and complete, just as you are. Even though there may be times when you encounter heavy storms and may feel as if the tides are not in your favor, forcing you to navigate turbulent waters, I want you to know that you have the strength within you to sail through those heavy storms safely ashore to the place within your very own existence called home.

You may have been feeling lost for a while, but know that was a necessary detour for your evolution, for your growth, and for your greatest comeback. Sisters and brothers, you were never meant to stay lost forever. Finding your way back home has always been your purpose. Believe in your magic and start stepping into your power. Shine your light. You're working so hard to believe that you are so small when you're actually massive. Brothers and sisters, those walls you built to protect you will no longer be necessary where you are heading. Trust that you are on the right path. The path to safety. The path to self-discovery and self-realization. The path to love. Brothers and Sisters, it's time to wake up from the illusion of separateness and realize that we are all one.

Acknowledgment

I extend my deepest gratitude to my partner, my children, and my dear friend Scott for introducing me to the transformative practice of meditation. Scott, your inspiration has been a guiding light.

A heartfelt thank you to my best friend, Yadira, from New York, who has been my unwavering support, encouraging me during moments of doubt and frustration. Yadira, I love you, sister.

Special appreciation goes to Donna, whose artistic talent brought the cover photo to life. Your creative touch added a unique dimension to my book.

I am immensely thankful to Iyamuremye for his invaluable support in shaping both this book and my journey toward becoming the better version of myself. Iyamuremye, your guidance has propelled me forward.

To all my friends and loved ones mentioned here, your presence in my life has made this endeavor possible. Thank you for being the pillars of encouragement and inspiration.

Contents

About The Author I

A Heartfelt Note II

Acknowledgment III

Introduction 1

Chapter 1: Who Am I? Who Are You? 7

Chapter 2: My Spiritual Awakening, Meeting My Higher Self 17

Chapter 3: My Childhood 30

Chapter 4: Moving To Canada 46

Chapter 5: New York 60

Chapter 6: Meeting My Karmic Partner 76

Chapter 7: Feeling Like A Maid 94

Chapter 8: Living With An Abusive Partner 116

Chapter 9: Fresh Start 128

Chapter 10: The End Of A Toxic Relationship 136

Chapter 11: The Unbearable 144

Chapter 12: The Healing Journey 154

Chapter 13: Everything Is Perspective 166

Introduction

I understand the feeling of powerlessness all too well. Five years ago, I hit rock bottom, overwhelmed by an excruciating emotional pain that left me clueless about how to ease it. I found myself questioning everything, even the very meaning of my existence. All I knew was that I desperately wanted the pain to disappear, even if it meant considering suicide as an option. I grappled with thoughts of ending my life every single day for several years. While I hid my suffering behind a mask, pretending to the world that I was okay, inside, I felt like I was enduring a relentless storm.

Despite the agony, I pushed forward for the sake of my family. But life intervened and said, "No more pretending, no more suffering." I was faced with a choice: to either end my life or to continue living, albeit in a profoundly different way from what I had known throughout my entire existence.

Deep in my heart, I held a conviction that life had more to offer than the dark, soul-draining, and painful reality I had created for myself. It was a moment of choice, and I opted for healing. I committed to finding the means to lead a more balanced, intentional, and serene life. Eventually, I discovered it. Through the practices of meditation and spirituality, I embarked on a journey that led me back to the realms of peace, love, and heightened awareness.

Through the passage of time, I've come to understand that nothing in life unfolds by coincidence. The universe has always been a guiding force, a protector, and a source of subtle signs. It was a realization that had eluded me in the past. Every experience and every person who crossed my path, whether their impact was "positive" or "negative," has been a valuable teacher. I've grown to cherish all these encounters because they have collectively brought me to this very moment.

Of course, I didn't always perceive life in this way. There were moments when I questioned our creator, wondering what I had done to deserve the pain and suffering I had faced. But in the grander scheme of things, these trials and tribulations have been instrumental in shaping the person I've become today.

For years, I found myself trapped in survival mode, wearing the heavy cloak of a victim mentality. I often wallowed in self-pity, drowning in a sea of anger and defensiveness. Chaos seemed to be my constant companion, trailing me wherever I ventured, leaving me breathless in its wake.

It wasn't until I carved out the space to sit with myself in silence that I truly grasped the turmoil within me, the unrestrained thoughts and emotions I had suppressed for so long. I became an observer of my own internal chaos, igniting a sense of curiosity to unearth the root causes of those thoughts and emotions.

You see, I had been labeled as the black sheep of the family, the one who became pregnant at 15 and was subsequently exiled from the house. I was the one who engaged in frequent high school fights, seemingly leaving a trail of chaos in my wake. I carried the weight of anger, feeling like an unwelcome burden wherever I went. The perspectives of others had sculpted this identity, and I had trapped myself within that confining box for far too long. One of the most formidable challenges I ever faced was summoning the courage to step into my vulnerability. It marked the turning point in my journey of self-discovery and personal transformation.

As I pen down this book, baring my shadows, recounting my darkest times, and revealing moments I'm not particularly proud of, I choose to embrace every emotion that emerges from the deepest part of my being. I shine the light of awareness on them all. I willingly place myself in a position of complete vulnerability by sharing my journey, and I do so with intention, a clear purpose, and an abundance of love.

Vulnerability is the thread that binds us and unites us as human beings. My story might serve as a beacon of hope in someone's life, no matter how small that glimpse may be. If that's all my story amounts to, I would have fulfilled the purpose intended by the source.

With utmost dedication, I offer this book to all the souls who have weathered or continue to weather challenging times. To these beautiful souls, I encourage you to tap into your vulnerability, to be genuine with yourself and your emotions, for it's in this vulnerability that the journey of healing begins. Healing is a priceless gift you can bestow upon yourself, your family, your friends, and the world. By embracing your imperfections, emotions, and shadows, you will ultimately find the peace you seek.

Recognize that you are complete and whole, just as you are. Through the practices of meditation and stillness, you will confront your insecurities, guilt, shame, dark thoughts, and ego.

Bring all of them into your conscious awareness. Become familiar with your limiting beliefs, patterns, and behaviors that may hinder your evolution into the best version of yourself. In this awareness, you'll start making peace with yourself, a gift equally enriching for you and the world at large.

Putting words together and expressing my feelings has always been challenging for me. The flow of words never came easily, and I often felt burdened by this difficulty. However, I have been called to confront this challenge, driven by a greater force compelling me to write and share my story.

I struggled to articulate my thoughts and feelings throughout my life, and the reasons behind this difficulty remain hidden from me. I carried the weight of feeling unintelligent, unworthy, and a perpetual failure. Consequently, I channeled my inward and outward frustration, wrestling with the inability to convey my inner world. It was only when I uncovered the profound impact of complex childhood trauma that I began to understand the connection between my experiences and my ability to acquire healthy coping mechanisms and constructive means of expressing and communicating my emotions.

My environment lacked the nurturing space that would have allowed me to freely articulate my thoughts and feelings. While the thoughts were present, they were stifled by intimidation, threats, and even actual violence. These early developmental milestones crucial for the formation of speech and thoughts were significantly curtailed. The constant stress I endured had detrimental effects on my brain and body, causing elevated cortisol levels and a broad range of impacts on my brain function- the amygdala, hippocampus, and the prefrontal cortex. These changes and elevated neurochemicals pushed me into a continuous fight-or-flight mode, locking me into a state of survival. Yet, there is a beacon of hope. I've discovered a transformative practice that enables the strengthening and restoration of the brain in ways once believed impossible. This practice is known as meditation. Meditation is profoundly linked to the phenomenon of neuroplasticity, rejuvenating cognitive functions, heightening self-awareness, and opening doors to higher dimensions of understanding and healing.

During a serene meditation, when I emerged fully into the present moment, I encountered and experienced a mystical force. The same higher intelligence that orchestrates the Earth's orbit around the Sun and the birth of new stars and galaxies. I refer to this intelligence as consciousness—the very heartbeat of existence. Remarkably, I discovered that this same consciousness resides within me and everyone.

Just as the universe is a dominion of chaos and polarity, so too are these elements woven into the fabric of your being. Much like the Earth's magnetic field can reverse its polarity, you possess the power of transformation. This concealed force directs the subatomic particles within atoms and guides our cells in fulfilling their role of providing structure and function. Yet, we have forgotten that this force dwells within us. We have been conditioned to believe in our separation from the heartbeat of life. The truth is you are an embodiment of the entire cosmos. Everything you seek is nestled within you, awaiting your choice to board on the journey of self-discovery. It's not about becoming something new but the reflective act of remembering who you truly are.

Chapter 1: Who Am I? Who Are You?

"If you can be absolutely comfortable with not knowing who you are, then what's left is who you are- being behind the human, a field of pure potentiality rather than something already defined. Give up defining yourself- to yourself and others. You won't die. You will come to life."

Eckhart Tolle

In the pages of my life's story, I've journeyed through the chapters of longing and yearning. As a young child, I clung to a dream, a wish for my parents' love and presence. Beside the window, I would sit, filled with anticipation, awaiting the day they'd come to find me, take me in their warm embraces, and softly utter those treasured words, "I love you." My heart throbbed for those instances, for the assurance of their affection.

Time flew by, and as I matured into an adult, I began questioning my selected partners. Why couldn't they see the real me? Why weren't they loving and romantic like I had hoped? It was during my self-reflection that I unearthed a profound truth. How could they discern my true essence when I, myself, failed to recognize my own value? The answer lay concealed within my own heart.

So, I waited. Years transitioned into seasons, and I clung to that longing for the deep love I yearned for. I craved the embrace from my parents and those romantic evenings with my partner, yet they remained perpetually elusive. It felt like I was chasing a mirage, an illusion that never materialized. Yet, the beauty of my story doesn't solely reside in the waiting but in the transformation that ensued. I learned that love, in its purest form, commences from within. During my journey of self-discovery, I chanced upon a significant revelation. I realized that the love I fervently sought from others, be it from my parents during my childhood or my partners in adulthood, was, in essence, a reflection of the love I needed to cultivate within myself. Life seemed as though its enduring wisdom had been gently steering me toward a pivotal lesson—my inner child needed healing.

In the process of mending these inner child wounds, I grasped a fundamental truth: it wasn't the people I encountered who needed to extend their love to me. However, life might have been simpler if I had found that love externally. It was, in the grander scheme of life, instructing me on how to love myself. It was teaching me the art of becoming my own foremost and genuine love.

With each stride I took along the path of self-discovery, I learned to nurture and console that wounded inner child. I discovered how to speak to her with tenderness, assuring her of her worthiness of love and happiness. It was a process of embracing my past, acknowledging the pain, and bestowing upon that little girl inside me the love and validation she had yearned for all those years.

As I continued to heal, the love I had sought externally began to emanate from within. I evolved into my primary source of love and encouragement. The void that had once consumed me gradually filled with self-compassion, self-acceptance, and a profound self-love that radiated from the depths of my being. Life's lessons, frequently disguised as trials and tribulations, became the catalyst for my personal transformation.

As my quest for self-love continued, I came to realize that this journey encompassed more than just embracing self-acceptance and nurturing my inner child; it was also a profound exploration to unearth the core of my true self. The question that had reverberated through my mind like an enduring refrain for years now demanded my full attention: Who am I?

For as far back as my memory stretches, this question has always been etched somewhere within me. It burdened my heart and left me grappling with an uncertain sense of identity. I often felt adrift, uncertain of where I truly belonged. Shuffled from one home to another, city to city, and even country to country, I experienced constant upheaval, leaving me feeling like a transient soul, someone who didn't quite fit anywhere.

Frequently, I couldn't shake the feeling that I was more of a burden than a cherished presence. This perception's weight haunted me and cast a shadow on my journey toward self-love. Yet, it was precisely within this crucible of uncertainty that I unearthed the strength to redefine myself.

With each step I took along this path, I began to peel back the layers of my identity. I delved into my passions, values, and the unique attributes that constituted me. It became a journey of introspection and self-discovery, where I learned to appreciate the difficult montage of experiences that had molded me.

In this process, I realized my past or external circumstances didn't confine me. Instead, I held the power to architect my own identity, to choose who I wanted to be. Embracing this newfound self-awareness, I found a sense of belonging within myself. The echoes of self-doubt and the feeling of being a burden slowly dissipated as I grew to love and accept the person I had become. It was a transformational voyage, leading me to understand that the most vital belonging I needed was to myself. Within my own embrace, I discovered profound love and acceptance that transcended the need for validation from external sources.

As I navigated through the different chapters of my life, I often caught myself attempting to conceal or downplay my true self in the hopes of fitting into new environments. Repeatedly, I would contort my identity, striving to fit into the molds I believed were anticipated of me. It felt as though I were donning various masks, each tailored to suit a particular role.

Yet, as I ventured further along the path of self-discovery, a shift began to transpire within me. I came to the realization that I no longer held any inclination to play the roles of the "nice girl" or the "good girl," as I had been conditioned to do. I had invested far too much time conforming to the expectations and judgments of others. It was akin to being cast in an unending performance, constantly aiming to please the audience and fulfill the expectations and perceptions of everyone else.

This awakening to my newfound realization brought about a sense of liberation and empowerment. I consciously chose to cast aside the layers of pretense and liberate myself from the bonds of people-pleasing. I understood that my authenticity held greater value than any role I had been striving to embody.

My expedition of self-discovery has transformed into an unwavering quest to peel away all the layers that do not define me. It's a process to cast aside the suffocating guise of the "good girl" that society had imposed upon me. I've reached a point where I hold no inclination to be anyone other than my authentic self. The pretenses and outward facades have grown wearisome, and I stand ready to reveal those dormant aspects of myself, eagerly awaiting their moment to shine.

Concealed beneath the veneer of societal norms and expectations lies a reservoir of identities that were once criticized by the world. The inner wild woman, the alchemist, the witch, the healer, the free spirit—all yearn to break free from the shackles of conformity and be unveiled to the world. These facets of my true self have waited patiently for their time to surface, and I'm resolute in allowing them to shine unapologetically.

I've come to comprehend that my true essence is not confined to external labels or societal roles. For much of my life, I was under the misguided notion that my identity was tethered to my name, my job title, my personality, or my current circumstances. If I were to ask you, "Who are you?" how would you respond? Often, we reduce our identity to our job titles, our achievements, our failures, our challenges, or even our traumas. We constrain ourselves to a set of characteristics, labels, and convictions about our identity.

However, the verity is that we transcend the limitations imposed by our minds. We are not merely the culmination of our past experiences, roles, or the judgments foisted upon us.

We are complex, multi-dimensional beings, each harboring a rich treasure of emotions, aspirations, and potential awaiting discovery. The depths of our being extend far beyond what our minds often lead us to believe. We constitute a mosaic of contrasting shades—love and fear, extroversion and introversion. Could it be that we exist as an endless realm of potentiality awaiting exploration without limits? Consider this: each life experience unfolds with a set of potential outcomes. Occasionally, life thrusts upon us unwanted or extraordinary experiences, ones that may stir the darkest aspects within us and leave us grappling with trauma. These experiences etch indelible imprints on our lives, challenging our prior self-identifications.

In the aftermath of such experiences, we begin to generate thoughts that diverge from the self-image we had cultivated in the past. We craft new narratives and self-perceptions grounded in the aftermath of our trials. Some of these thoughts may resonate with those we had once judged in others or suppressed within ourselves. Yet, these very thoughts arise as a consequence of our experiences.

Now, the most important question is: do we permit these novel thoughts to mold a fresh identity for us? Do we become fascinated by the belief that this is the "new" us, forever altered by our experiences? Or do we embark on a journey of reinvention, a voyage of rediscovery and reclamation of our authentic selves?

The choice lies within our grasp. We wield the power to author our own narrative and define our own identity. We can employ our experiences as catalysts for growth, forging a more robust, resilient iteration of ourselves. In doing so, we embrace the infinite possibilities residing within us, recognizing that our identity is not a static entity but a perpetually evolving masterpiece. So, for those contemplating their path of self-discovery and grappling with the reverberations of life's experiences, bear in mind that you wield the brush to paint your identity. You are not confined by the past or the judgments of others. Seize the authority to reinvent yourself, explore the limitless potential within, and craft a narrative that harmonizes with the true essence of your being. Your journey is a canvas, and you are the artist who can choose to compose a masterpiece.

I wholeheartedly concur that our perception of self should remain in a perpetual state of evolution, continually adapting and expanding as we traverse different phases of life. We should welcome the emergence of a new self sculpted by our ever-evolving experiences. However, what truly resonates as profound is the recognition that our core essence, our very being, extends far beyond the confines of identity.

The profound truth lies in our status as spiritual beings navigating human experiences within these physical vessels. Our existence transcends the limitations of our mortal bodies. We are complex beings composed of trillions of cells engaged in an interplay of minerals, elements, and water. We maintain a connection with the very fabric of the universe.

Ponder this: you are intertwined with fungi, plants, rocks, atoms, and stardust. You echo the cosmic origins of the universe itself. In your essence, you are delicately interlinked with nature. You exist not as a separate entity but as a part of the world's existence.

Moreover, you are an embodiment of the divine. You are a manifestation of the sacred, and so is everything else. The universal consciousness, the energy that courses through every atom, every living entity, is a facet of this grand divine medley. We are not isolated individuals but rather unique expressions of universal consciousness, experiencing life through the lens of individuality. In this profound realization, we come to comprehend that the constraints of identity are precisely that— constraints. Our true nature is expansive, limitless, and profoundly linked to the cosmos. We are part of a greater whole, reflecting the divine energy that permeates the universe.

Self-discovery, the profound journey of uncovering one's true essence, often requires a transformative cocoon phase. This stage is typically evaded, for it is anything but straightforward; it's a messy and bewildering part of the process. It's the phase where you cease to be the caterpillar but have yet to become the butterfly. It's the transitional pupa stage of your transformation.

During this cocoon phase, a profound shift takes place. You become enveloped in confusion, questioning every aspect of your existence and encountering what can only be described as an identity crisis. It's a puzzling period, a time when the old constructs of your self-perception cease to serve their purpose, and you teeter on the brink of something new and unknown.

At this stage, it becomes paramount to allow yourself to unravel and submit to the process. Your soul is beckoning for transformation, and it's time to dismantle all the versions of yourself that you had constructed for the sake of survival. It's an act of release, letting go, and permitting those outdated versions of you to fade away, for it's through this dissolution that rebirth becomes attainable. Keep in mind that this phase is a natural facet of your evolution, and every fiber of your being yearns for this transformation. It's the stage at which you shed the layers that no longer serve you, creating room for something new to emerge. It's not just about evolving into a better version of yourself; it's about becoming your true self, discarding the illusions, and embracing your authentic essence. For anyone traversing this cocoon phase of self-discovery, recognize that you're amidst a beautiful and necessary transformation. Embrace the confusion, the queries, and the discomfort. Permit yourself to unravel because, in this process of relinquishing and surrendering, you will ultimately discover the freedom to be reborn, to emerge as the genuine butterfly that has always resided within you. Your soul yearns for this transformation, and it's an extraordinary, awe-inspiring journey of self-realization.

Throughout my life, I've witnessed countless deaths and subsequent rebirths. In each instance, I surrendered a little deeper, even when the process of shedding the old self was veiled in fear and uncertainty. It's as if, with every transformation, I consciously forged a sacred space within myself to bear witness to the graceful dissolution of my former self, making room for the emergence of a more evolved, more authentic self.

The demise of my previous self and the birthing of my genuine, authentic self marked a profound odyssey of self-discovery. It unveiled the exhilarating truth that shedding layers of conditioning and societal expectations ushered in a profound sense of euphoria. It was akin to being intoxicated by the sheer beauty of life itself. I began to savor life more deeply, relishing the richness of each moment.

Throughout this process, I gained a profound comprehension of the timeless verity that reality is perpetually present in the now. The essence of existence weaves itself into the depths of the present moment. A deep-seated knowing dawned upon me:

we are all intimately interconnected, sharing the same cosmic thread of consciousness. As this realization unfurled, I grasped the significance of healing and the release of pain, recognizing that it was through healing that I elevated my vibrational frequency.

The elevation of this energetic frequency extended its influence far beyond me—it radiated outward, setting off a ripple effect that traversed the universe. Those in close proximity and, indeed, the broader world felt the reverberations of my transformation. I became an influential force, possessing a potency beyond my wildest imaginings.

To those who have boarded on the profound voyage of self-discovery, embrace each instance of death and rebirth. They serve as the stepping stones leading you to your genuine, authentic self. As you ascend to higher states of consciousness, you metamorphose into a beacon of light, disseminating healing and love to all you touch. You become a catalyst for positive change, and the reach of your influence knows no bounds. In your authenticity and personal evolution, you hold the power to transform not only yourself but also the very world.

Chapter 2: My Spiritual Awakening, Meeting My Higher Self

As I sat in silence, immersed in my usual meditation practice, something shifted. It was an extraordinary moment marked by a surge of energy coursing through every fiber of my being, a powerful possession of body and soul unlike anything I had ever felt before. The intensity was unparalleled. Swirls of colors swarmed before my eyes, and I sensed a profound transformation blossoming. Yet, confusion gripped me—what was happening to me?

In this paradox of emotions, I found myself teetering between two extremes. On the one hand, a wave of complete bliss and peace permeated every core of my being. I could feel the pain in my body starting to loosen its grip, simultaneously releasing its hold on every cell within me. This was a moment of deep mystery and revelation, an experience that went beyond the ordinary.

As I ventured into this unfamiliar territory, the contrast between bliss and the cathartic release of pain became the defining features of my journey. In that sacred moment, I found myself suspended between the known and the unknown, guided by the currents of energy that flowed through me, orchestrating a ballet of profound healing and self-discovery.

During this intense experience, my head throbbed, and a heavy feeling overwhelmed me. Sensations of tingling and vibrations coursed through my entire being, akin to a mild electric shock. Strangely, I found myself perceiving auras everywhere, adding to the surreal nature of the moment. Suddenly, a thought flashed—could this be a stroke? Despite all that, I sensed the warmth of something mystical enveloping me, though it remained elusive to my eyes, visible only to my heightened senses. Conflicted, my rational side, influenced by my nurse instincts, urged me to consider visiting the hospital. This didn't feel normal. The clash between the mystical sensations and the practical voice within me created a strange and perplexing moment where the boundaries between the tangible and the unseen blurred.

The headaches lingered for about another week, though thankfully not as intense as that initial episode. Seeking answers, I turned to the internet and discovered a surprising revelation—I wasn't alone in my experiences. Numerous people were reporting similar symptoms. It appeared that many were undergoing a profound awakening, connecting with higher consciousness, and encountering their higher selves and spirit guides through meditation. This realization shifted my perspective, transforming what initially felt like an isolated and bewildering incident into a shared journey of self-discovery and higher connection.

The persistent headaches unveiled a profound transformation—I realized my pineal gland was activated. From that day forward, my perception of the world underwent a seismic shift. Colors became more vivid, the world more vibrant and alive. Birdsong, once background noise, now resonated with newfound clarity. This heightened awareness compelled me to pay attention to details I had previously overlooked, as if I had been living my entire life in a haze, now experiencing reality with fresh, unhindered eyes. The change went beyond sensory perception. A deep sense of love and peace flourished within me, accompanied by a yearning for unity. It felt as though I was seamlessly connected with the entire universe, transcending time constraints. That day marked the realization that life and existence hold depths far beyond my prior knowledge and beliefs. A mystical world opened before me, beckoning to be discovered—an experience akin to removing virtual reality goggles and unveiling a more profound and enchanting reality than I had ever imagined.

Higher Self

In the journey of self-discovery, I delved into the concept of the higher self, an aspect of our being that transcends the limitations of the everyday mind. It's essentially the wiser, higher mind within us—the true essence of who we are.

Think of it as your light body, your spirit, your intuition—a reservoir of boundless love, bliss, confidence, clarity, curiosity, and safety. This version of you, vibrating at the highest frequency, is free from limitations, fears, or past traumas. It is the spirit of your highest vibration, forever connected to the divine.

As I discovered that each one of us is a fragment of the divine, I embarked on a deep journey to connect with my higher self. This exploration has led me to realize that the more time we spend with our higher self, the more we align with its elevated frequency. Through the practice of silence, meditation, and conscious breathing, we unlock the gateway to this transformative connection. This journey has been nothing short of a revelation—a shedding of layers that bound me to fears and insecurities. As I embraced my higher self, I found a reservoir of strength and wisdom within, a guiding force leading me toward a life fueled by love, purpose, and harmony. It's a journey that unearths the dormant potential within, a journey toward becoming the highest, most authentic version of oneself. Through the calmness of silence and the serenity of meditation, I discovered the divine connection within, unlocking a wellspring of resilience, joy, and profound understanding.

On the flip side, there exists the lower self, the voice of the ego mind—the part of us that aims to shield but unconsciously constrains. It's the persistent whisper in our thoughts, insinuating that we're not "good enough," fostering self-sabotage as a misguided shield from potential embarrassment or fear of being seen. It's the habitual aspect that clings to the familiar, fearing change and resisting growth. The ego is the story we create about ourselves and the identity we have attached to ourselves. It's like being stuck in a rut, afraid of change, and too comfortable with what we already know. It's the story we tell ourselves about who we are, even if it's not always true.

To achieve a harmonious flow with the universe, it's important to align with both the higher self and the lower self. This journey isn't about suppressing the lower self but rather understanding it, acknowledging its fears, and guiding it toward a more liberated state. By balancing the wisdom of the higher self and the protective instincts of the lower self, a magical connection is formed. Embracing both aspects allowed me to experience a more holistic and authentic connection with the universe.

Let's be clear about one thing. The transformation isn't about shunning the lower self; it's about transcending its limitations. It's a journey of self-awareness and compassionate self-dialogue, paving the way for an integrated existence where the higher and lower selves coexist, fostering a profound alignment with the rhythm of the universe. The genesis of my spiritual journey started the moment I summoned the courage to face myself—to take on an introspective path, exploring the recesses of my deepest inner shadows. It was a weighty decision to question everything about life and reality, including the negative thinking patterns and triggers that had long held sway over my existence.

This journey compelled me to revisit my past, to confront head-on those traumatic moments that had cast a heavy shadow on my being. With an untiring commitment to courage and love, I approached this contemplation with a non-judgmental lens. Each step was laden with self-analysis, peeling back layers with a gentle yet determined touch.

In facing the echoes of my past, I discovered that the wounds carried deep lessons, and the healing process wasn't about erasing the scars but understanding their significance. It became a sacred exploration, a pilgrimage within, where I unearthed the resilience to confront my deepest fears and the compassion to embrace every facet of my being.

Well, this journey was not without its challenges, yet my commitment to facing the shadows of my past altered each hurdle into a stepping stone. It was in this exploration that I discovered the power of self-love—a force capable of changing darkness into light. This quest, marked by introspection and self-discovery, paved the way for spiritual conversion, reshaping my perception of life, reality, and the bond that binds us all. Thinking about my journey, I remembered some very heart-touching lines I read in a book. It said:

"The greatest damage done by neglect, trauma or emotional loss is not the immediate pain they inflict but the long-term distortions they induce in the way a developing child will continue to interpret the world and her situation in it. All too often, these ill-conditioned implicit beliefs become self-fulfilling prophecies in our lives. We create meanings from our unconscious interpretation of early events, and then we forge our present experiences from the meaning we've created. Unwittingly, we write the story of our future from narratives based on the past...Mindful awareness can bring into consciousness those hidden, past-based perspectives so that they no longer frame our worldview.' Choice begins the moment you disidentify from the mind and its conditioned patterns, the moment you become present...Until you reach that point, you are unconscious.' ...In present awareness, we are liberated from the past."

Gabor Maté, In the Realm of Hungry Ghosts:

Close Encounters with Addiction

Life before my spiritual awakening was an emotional rollercoaster, oscillating between the desire to survive and the tempting allure of giving up. The shift occurred when I started to engage in the act of sitting in silence—a surrender to the cacophony of my emotions and thoughts. In that serene space, I unearthed the realization that I didn't need to wrestle with my emotions; instead, I could surrender to them. It was a shift from the notion of giving up to giving in—an acceptance of all those emotions and thoughts I had meticulously avoided. To observe and feel them without judgment became my mantra, fostering a deep stillness within. This stillness, I recognized, was the gateway to the "I am" presence—an unfiltered connection with the essence of my being. The transformation, the alteration of my existence, manifested when I acknowledged that the beliefs I held were the very threads weaving the fabric of my reality. It was a profound understanding that what I chose to believe in dictated the power I bestowed upon it. This revelation marked a departure from the tumultuous rollercoaster of survival instincts to a serene journey of self-discovery, where the simple act of surrendering to the present moment unveiled a reflective inner peace and a newfound sense of empowerment.

I would sincerely suggest that to catalyze a positive transformation in your life, begin the journey of changing your thoughts. Refuse to grant power to thoughts that do not align with your highest purpose or serve your well-being. Recognize that within you lies the potential to experience the divine and embody love—a purpose for which you were inherently born.

In this cosmic existence, abundance is not a distant dream but your birthright. Shifting your mindset to accept this truth opens the door to a life steeped in abundance. It's a conscious choice to resonate with the frequency of love and richness, a choice that ripples outward, reciprocating positivity and prosperity to the outer world.

If given the chance to converse with my younger self, I would embrace her tightly, conveying my immense pride in her untiring determination. I would remind her that the journey ahead will be arduous, but she possesses the strength to surmount any challenge.

I would tell her that life is often unjust, dealing us with difficult hands. It is within these moments that our true resilience and fortitude are revealed. The trials she faced, I would emphasize, were not without purpose; they were shaping her into the person she was destined to become. I would assure her that mistakes are a natural part of growth and that vulnerability is where we truly discover ourselves. I would stress that self-love is essential, and she should never allow anyone to diminish her worth. And I would encourage her to understand the world - it can be harsh but also brimming with beauty and wonder. I urge her to explore, learn, and embrace all life offers. I would accentuate that all her passions and dreams are worth pursuing relentlessly.

I would acknowledge that the road ahead will be challenging, but she is not alone. A support system surrounds her, filled with deep love and care. I would assure her that it is okay to seek assistance and lean on others when needed.

I would affirm that she is a warrior, an unyielding force, and nothing can hinder her from achieving her aspirations. I would emphasize that the world yearns for her unique voice and perspective. I would urge her to radiate her light boldly, never allowing it to dim for anyone.

If granted the opportunity to address my younger self, I would convey all of this and more. I would reaffirm her worth, her value, and her significance. Above all, I would stress that she is enough just as she is.

What makes my heart swell with pride is not just her ability to navigate those adversities but the fierce courage she wielded in the absence of ample knowledge, understanding, or the tools to guide her through the tumultuous terrain. I would appreciate her resilience that, amidst doubts that echoed in the corridors of a critical world and the painful echo of self-criticism, a radiant spark within her refused to flicker out. It ignited a relentless pursuit for a version of herself she believed in, a better version, one molded by the trials she faced. I stand in awe of her resilience, a quality that transformed her falls into lessons and her wounds into wisdom. In acknowledging her internal battles, battles that forced her to her knees, I marvel at her ability to rise like a true warrior. Each time she confronted fears, challenges, and traumas, she gazed unflinchingly into their eyes, declaring with a loud boom, "No more, enough is enough." It's a proclamation that echoes through the corridors of time, a battle cry that signals the end of suffering.

I'm not just proud of her; I'm profoundly moved by the strength she embodied. In the vast expanse of the universe, the strongest souls are indeed dispatched to the darkest corners, and she, my younger self, emerged as a beacon of light, illuminating those very shadows. Her journey, marked by falls and rises, is a testament to the indomitable spirit within. If I could tell her one thing, it would be a heartfelt acknowledgment: "You did it. The suffering ends here."

In the present moment, if someone asked me about my soul's deepest yearning, the resounding response would echo the word "freedom." It's a craving for true freedom—a liberation that extends beyond the conventional boundaries of life.

This yearning encompasses the freedom to self-express authentically, unrestricted by societal norms or expectations. It craves the liberty to wholeheartedly pursue all my passions and desires, unburdened by limitations or external constraints. It's a desire for the freedom to traverse the world to explore its diverse landscapes and cultures with an unrestrained spirit. This soulful longing extends to the freedom to choose my dwelling place anywhere on this planet, free from the shackles of geographical restrictions. It's an aspiration to live life on my terms, to embrace the vastness of possibilities and experiences that the world offers, unrestricted by conservative boundaries.

Honestly, I spent most of my life enveloped in a fog. The healing journey, I've come to realize, is far from an easy path. The prevalence of sadness and anger and the alarming rise in suicide and mental illness underscore the challenging nature of this odyssey. Healing trauma isn't a quick fix; it demands considerable effort, a willingness to navigate a myriad of emotions, and a commitment to self-reflection that delves into the shadowy recesses of one's inner being.

Embarking on this journey necessitates the readiness to confront fears and unravel suppressed emotions. It beckons a crucial question: Are you prepared to meet yourself? Because, if so, the healing journey reveals like an expedition to the depths of your soul, areas neglected and yearning for your awareness. These are the profound, dark corners within your being, seeking the warmth of your love and the brilliance of your light.

Your shadow self, often overlooked or even feared, is an integral part of your existence deserving of love and awareness, just like any other facet of your being. Many attempt to circumvent the struggles, unknowingly missing the vital lessons hidden within them. The healing journey, though challenging, becomes a transformative pilgrimage, guiding you toward the neglected recesses of your soul, where growth and self-discovery await.

Power of Meditation and Spirituality

As I narrate my story within the pages of this book, the spotlight has consistently shone on the transformative powers of meditation and spirituality—forces that have woven threads of profound impact throughout my life. Let me share with you how these potent tools, like alchemists of the soul, have transmuted my existence in ways I could have never fathomed in my wildest dreams.

Meditation, a gentle yet potent force, has forged resilient pathways within the expanse of my brain, fostering self-awareness, enhancing memory, honing learning capabilities, and harmonizing emotional regulation. In the wake of this transformation, mental clarity has become a cherished companion, manifesting as a notable boost in cognitive skills. The once scattered fragments of my speech and thoughts have now coalesced into a more coherent expression, unveiling an improved articulation that reverberates through newfound confidence.

My senses have heightened, reaching levels I hadn't thought possible. The calming embrace of meditation has extended to my sympathetic nervous system, orchestrating an experience that not only reduces anxiety but also eradicates the haunting specters of panic attacks and depression. Beyond personal revelation, scientific studies stand as testaments to the manifold benefits of meditation. Research shows that eight weeks of consistent mindful meditation has the potential to help people recover from addiction, unveiling a path to liberation. Delving deeper into the realms of science, the profound effects of consistent meditation are underscored by neuroplasticity—a transformative phenomenon that extends to reducing age-related brain degeneration. In the core of my being, I now resonate with a profound sense of aliveness, a richness that surpasses any previous chapters of my existence. Through the lens of meditation and spirituality, I've discovered a life more vibrant and fuller than ever before.

Meditation, a profound journey for me, acts as the key to unlocking the door to spirituality and connecting me with my higher self and spirit guides. Entering a meditative state, I feel transported to an ocean of love, peace, and unity, where everything melds into one. This awe-inspiring place, saturated with pure consciousness, love, and oneness, enfolds me in tranquility and a sense of belonging.

Within this meditation sanctum, I've unearthed a wellspring of wisdom and guidance akin to a treasure trove of insight and intuition that has forged new pathways in my life. My intuition has flourished, deepening my connection to the universe and everyone within it. This heightened connection has given me a clearer understanding of my life's purpose, instilling in me a sense of direction and purpose previously unexperienced. Embracing the present moment, I've found solace and empowerment in the here and now.

Meditation is a gateway to altered states of consciousness, offering experiences like remote viewing. Through this, I've encountered powerful, insightful visions and discovered an enhanced sense of foresight and prophecy. A whole new world has opened before me, one where the boundaries of reality blur, and I can tap into a deep understanding of the world around me.

Through breathwork and meditation, I've experienced the release of DMT, often called 'the spirit molecule.' This has enabled me to dig into mystical states of consciousness, revealing the boundless nature of our realities. It's a realization that fills me with awe and wonder, recognizing that the limitations we perceive are mere illusions.

This transformative journey imbued me with a profound sense of purpose, connection, and understanding. It awakens a deep motivation, inspiring me to continue exploring the depths of my spirituality and the boundless potential within. The emotional impact is immeasurable, filling my heart with peace, purpose, and wonder that accompanies me daily.

Chapter 3: My Childhood

Before diving deeper into this journey of reflection, I would like to say that every life story mirrors the facets of a diamond, emerging from the depths of roughness to radiate brilliance. Let's rewind to the beginning, to the genesis of my tale, where, like any ordinary human being, I started as a child, paving the way for the chapters that would follow.

The canvas of my early childhood is painted with hues of love and happiness, set against the backdrop of Honduras. Born to parents whose maturity was yet to catch up with the responsibility of raising a child, my mom, at 17, and my dad, at 19, embarked on the journey of parenthood. Despite the challenges, my arrival was met with unconditional love and desire.

I was born into a world where my existence was not a mere happenstance. I was a child wanted and cherished, underscoring the depth of my parent's love and care for their child.

As young parents, they earnestly endeavored to provide the best they could, navigating the path of parenthood armed with limited knowledge and resources. In the crucible of their dedication, the foundation of my story was laid, etched with the raw sincerity of their efforts and the purity of their love.

In the chapters of my early years, the story took a turn as my parents' marriage, which had blossomed before my arrival, wilted within a mere three years. Before long, my father embarked on a journey to Canada as a refugee, leaving behind the landscapes of Honduras. At the tender age of five, I found myself anchored to the familiar embrace of my mother and grandparents in the land I called home.

My mother, a spirited woman with a zest for life, grappled with a demanding job at a newspaper company that demanded her presence across various corners of Honduras. Her sporadic returns brought moments of pure joy into my world. Her contagious spirit, infused with a love for revelry, painted my childhood with bursts of happiness. I cherished those times when she used to come back home. In her presence, I felt the warmth of happiness.

Despite the challenges of distance and her demanding job, my mother had an extraordinary energy that radiated joy. In her pursuit of joy, she embraced a lifestyle that defied the societal norms of her time. I still remember how my father often recounted tales of her free spirit, a woman unafraid to dance to the beat of her own drum during the vibrant era of the 1980s.

In a society where conformity prevailed, my mother dared to live with a freedom that set her apart. She was a woman of her own kind. She explored the world of drugs, with cannabis being her companion.

I vividly recall that evening when we visited one of her friends' house parties. The air was thick with a sense of liberation, perhaps fueled by the intoxicating melodies of Madonna echoing through the room. As the night passed by, laughter intertwined with the beats and liquor, creating a tableau of freedom and celebration in defiance of societal expectations.

Our humble abode in Honduras nestled into the embrace of a single-story house, a haven shared with my grandparents and my mom's siblings, an aunt, and an uncle. In the heart of a lower-middle-class neighborhood, we lacked opulence and extravagance, but what graced our home were the essentials of life and, more profoundly, an abundance of love.

Within those walls, love flowed freely, an undeniable force from my grandparents, my aunt, and my uncle. My mother, in her intermittent returns, showered me with affection that resonated deeply. Within the simplicity of our existence, the warmth of love painted our everyday moments.

The course of my life took a decisive turn when I learned that my father had won custody, aiming to bring me to Canada. However, the process would take a few years for him to secure permanent residency. In the interim, a different plan was designed for me. He decided it would be best for me to move to New York first to live with either his sister or brother, ensuring I could start learning English right away.

In my memories, I see the threads of my mother's love woven into the fabric of my early years. Her affection was my sanctuary, a place where her warmth, hugs, and smile cushioned me in comfort. She left no gaps in my upbringing, pouring her love into every corner of my existence. Her presence, a balm to my soul, soothed me from the inside out.

I cherished every moment spent with her, knowing she tried her best for me. Her love, delivered in her own unique way, was palpable in every interaction. Yet, amidst this undeniable love, an unspoken question lingered, echoing through the corridors of my mind for years. When did the currents of her love alter course? How does a mother, the center of a child's world, advocate for a seven-year-old to embark on a solitary journey to a foreign land, encouraging her to live amongst strangers? The perplexity of her assurances that I would be okay in this unfamiliar chapter without the presence of anyone I had ever known or loved haunted my thoughts, leaving an unanswered question that echoed in the chambers of my heart.

As young parents, my mother and father steered a myriad of choices, from providing for me to deciding on parenting styles, selecting the right school, and shaping the environment for my upbringing. But out of all these decisions, one of the most agonizing for my mother was the choice to let me go.

The depths of her truth and the reasons behind agreeing to send me to live with complete strangers in a foreign land remain veiled, forever locked away as she died in 2009.

The secrets buried in her heart and the layers of her intentions may forever elude my understanding, but deep within, I sense that her decision, however challenging, was made with the best intentions.

The vivid memory of the meticulous preparation for my U.S. visa remains etched in my mind. For weeks, my mother coached me on what to say and how to respond to the immigration officers at the U.S. consulate. I vividly recall her instructing me,

"You simply tell them you're visiting your aunts and uncle in New York. That's all they need to know."

Little did my seven-year-old self realize that the fate of this journey would hinge on a single stamp on my passport, an approval or denial that rested in the hands of beings beyond my control. Anyway, at the age of seven, I embarked on this new adventure, moving to New York to live with my uncle and his family.

Arriving in New York, I confronted a fear I had never known. I found myself distanced from everyone and everything I held dear. In the first few weeks, I resided at my aunt's house in Plattekill, NY, with my dad's sister. Then, I was shifted to my uncle's house. Recalling the emotions, it felt as if I were a heavy burden. This subsequent shift to my uncle's house introduced a sense of weightiness, as if I were a heavy burden, grappling with the unfamiliarity of my surroundings.

There I stood, alone in a stranger's home, with an uncle I barely knew. Our encounters had been limited to a single visit when he came to Honduras.

"Well, come in," he said. "Go look inside. You have another cousin around your age, and she will be home soon from school." Although he didn't say much to me, the air felt heavier. Despite the silence, the atmosphere seemed to thicken around me. It was as if the very air was closing in, suffocating me with an unknown force. The surroundings felt almost hostile, as if they were resisting my very presence, and the walls seemed to creep ever closer, threatening to crush me.

The anticipation of meeting this cousin felt like an eternity. Seated in the unfamiliar living room, I stared at the TV, tuned to a language I couldn't comprehend. Lost once again, a sense of isolation engulfed me. All I wished for was to cry, but that day, for some inexplicable reason, tears eluded me. I sat there in a daze, my throat dry from unshed tears and my chest weighed down with a heavy burden.

As I sat there, feeling misplaced, the creak of the front door caught my attention. From there walked in a skinny girl with dark hair.

"Hi, you," I greeted in Spanish.

"Do you want to play with me?" She responded with a simple smile, but her eyes held a depth that intrigued me.

There was a shared sense of loss and sadness between us. Her name was Aria, and in that instant, a connection sparked between two souls navigating the unfamiliar.

In the months that followed, the bond between Aria and me strengthened. We became inseparable, sharing our joys and sorrows. Aria, my uncle's stepchild, had a tumultuous past. Her mother, my aunt, departed Honduras when Aria was a baby, leaving her in the care of a compassionate woman unrelated by blood but who raised her with love and care. Like me, Aria had made the journey to New York at the tender age of seven, residing there for about a year before my arrival.

Her story was laced with layers of pain. My aunt, Aria's mother, carried the weight of her own traumatic upbringing. Unable to regulate her emotions, she unleashed her repressed anger on Aria, subjecting her to years of verbal, physical, and emotional mistreatment. Aria bore the scars of this mistreatment, yet her resilience and the warmth in her eyes spoke of a spirit determined to rise above the darkness.

In the cramped household, my aunt and uncle had two daughters of their own. Aria and I, at the tender ages of seven and eight, found ourselves thrust into the roles of seasoned caregivers adept at preparing milk bottles and changing diapers. The routine was interrupted only by the presence of a live-in nanny who assisted with cleaning and cared for the girls during the week. However, weekends brought a different dynamic. Before going outside to play, we were tasked with ensuring the house was clean, and the girls were fed.

Weekends were fraught with tension. If the house wasn't spotless or a detail overlooked, playtime was replaced with a harrowing ritual. Aria, my cousin, bore the brunt of her mother's anger. My aunt wielded anything within reach, inflicting physical punishment on Aria for perceived transgressions. Bruises and marks adorned her body as painful reminders of this routine. I, a helpless witness, sat through the ordeal, absorbing Aria's tears, screams, and pleas for mercy. The sound of the belt striking her fragile frame echoed through the house, leaving an indelible imprint of fear and heartbreak. It was a scene that etched a profound sense of powerlessness and anguish in my young heart.

In those early days, the tears would stream down my face each time my cousin faced the wrath of her mother. However, my cries were swiftly stifled, silenced by the looming threat of a similar fate for myself. Gradually, I devised a way to cope – a desperate attempt to shield myself from the brutality. I would close my eyes tightly, cover my ears, and pretend, in vain, that I wasn't there at all. The desire to vanish, to escape the harsh reality, consumed me. Yet, no matter how hard I tried to distance myself, I remained painfully present. After each brutal episode, my only solace was to envelop my poor cousin in a comforting hug. The relentless cycle of witnessing her suffering became a torment I couldn't escape, etching a profound sense of helplessness and sorrow into my young soul.

My connection with my aunt was a bit different. She mostly left me to my own devices while she dealt with her own unresolved pain and traumas. As I reflect, I understand that she, too, was an unhealed soul, a victim of abuse with her own scars to bear.

Within her, though, existed a softer, nurturing side. Beneath the surface of her struggles, she was caring and fun. Choosing to take me in and attempting to raise me as her own child demonstrated a depth of love that I've carried with me. Despite her own unhealed wounds, she made a genuine effort to provide me with a sense of belonging.

My uncle, too, carried the weight of unaddressed trauma and repressed anger, which he kept to himself. He ventured to New York alone as a teenager, carrying a heavy baggage of emotional wounds with him into this new, unfamiliar setting. He frequently lashed out at those closest to him, a typical response to unresolved pain. His strict demeanor was his way of coping.

Every morning meant a two-block walk to catch the bus to school. At 7.5 years old, I navigated the streets of one of New York's most perilous cities. There was this one day when I missed the bus. His anger welled up, and I found myself standing in the corner, sentenced to hours of silence, my gaze fixed on the wall. It was a minor punishment in the spectrum of what lay ahead.

Uncle's methods of discipline were varied, each etching its memory in my young mind. Kneeling on hard floors with arms raised became a routine, sometimes aggravated by the discomfort of rice strewn on the ground. Sometimes, we endured this position for hours. His watchful eyes ensured compliance, and I still remember how, in his absence, we'd seize those fleeting moments to lower our arms, seeking momentary relief from the burning pain. These were the struggles etched into the daily fabric of my existence.

However, it was not the end. The haunting echoes of abuse reverberated beyond physical torment. The resonance of name-calling and relentless yelling etched an indelible imprint on the fabric of my being, marking an emotional battleground that proved among the most formidable traumas to overcome.

Within the storm of anger, my uncle wielded a weapon of dehumanization, coining the term "bemba de Negra," translating to "N" lips in English. This racial insult was rooted in a distorted notion of superiority, as he falsely saw himself aligned with a supposedly superior race. Unbeknownst to him, my lineage bore the richness of African ancestry, a heritage he ignored.

His warped perception of racial superiority, influenced by a deluded sense of whiteness, clashed with the truth of my heritage. My ancestors were Black, a fact known through the lineage of my mother. This degrading label became a subconscious tool, ingraining a sense of inferiority within me. His words wove a narrative of inferiority into my young mind, an unspoken programming that sought to diminish my sense of dignity in comparison to White individuals. As he hurled those words, the damage wasn't just to my ears; it was a subtle act of programming that sought to distort my self-worth, a distortion woven into the very fabric of my identity.

The echoes of this verbal abuse lingered in the recesses of my mind, sowing a seed of self-doubt that would haunt me for years. For many years, I found it difficult to truly love myself. The struggle to embrace self-love manifested in peculiar ways, as even the choice of lipstick became a battleground. Red, with its boldness, carried a weight of discomfort, a fear of accentuating what had been labeled as "too much." Even as an adult, I would avoid wearing red lipstick because I was self-conscious about making my lips look bigger.

What often eludes our awareness is the profound impact of each scream, each name hurled at a child, and each instance of verbal or physical abuse. Over time, it's not just an assault on the body; it becomes a corrosive force that eats away at the soul. Power, voice, and authenticity—all casualties in the wake of such destructive patterns. For me, the toll was severe, leading to a loss of voice and authenticity.

As an adult, I grappled with articulating thoughts and expressing emotions, a stark departure from my childhood in Honduras, where communication flowed effortlessly. The persistent struggle left me questioning my own intelligence. It was a revelation that unfolded with time— trauma had been the underlying influence shaping my silence and self-doubt, transforming my path toward self-acceptance and healing. By reminiscing about my challenges and pains, my intentions are not to find faults. My intent is not to cast blame but to illuminate how trauma casts a long shadow over our behaviors, shaping the intricate patterns of our thoughts. Trauma's silent inheritance echoes through generations, weaving a thread that links our past to our present. Passed down through generations, trauma becomes a silent legacy, a cycle yearning to be broken. And breaking this cycle is our responsibility—a commitment to healing.

To disrupt this cycle, we must embark on a journey of self-discovery and inner healing. This path demands a courageous confrontation with our self-destructive patterns and a deep exploration of how they ripple into our relationships and the world around us. Emotional intelligence, especially for those scarred by childhood trauma, becomes an ongoing quest.

As I pen down these words, emotions surge, triggering an avalanche of unprocessed grief. My chest tightens with the weight of a seven-year-old who felt the world collapse around her. The echoes of her loneliness reverberate through time.

My inner child beckons to be heard, to express the pain that has long lingered unspoken. Despite almost three years of intense inner child wound healing and meditation, the act of writing reignites these dormant emotions. A familiar ache settles in my chest, a poignant reminder of a past I am revisiting.

In the sanctuary of meditation, I confront my inner child. I listen to the echoes of her cries, embracing her tightly. She must know she is safe to express, safe to feel. The journey isn't about erasing the past; it's about rewriting the narrative, letting her know she was never alone and that safety now envelopes her every expression. Let me take a moment to share some heartfelt words with the people my younger self deeply cared about from the bottom of her heart. The next few paragraphs are dedicated to those precious souls whom she wanted to connect with, to express the emotions and feelings that were close to her heart but remained unspoken. To those whom she wanted to reach out to but was never able to do so. To the most dear people in her life, for whom she wanted to pour her heart, these words are for you.

To my uncle, these are the whispers of my inner child:

Do you see me, uncle? Hear me in the silent echoes of my past? Feel the yearning for your love that lingered unanswered? Love – a language foreign to your own heart, shrouded in the struggles you bore behind the façade you wore. Was that why you couldn't say those three words I longed to hear? Were they trapped in the fortress you built around yourself?

Uncle, your struggles were engraved on your heart, scars that painted your journey in self-unkindness. Did your own battles make it hard to open your heart, to let love in? The words "I love you" lingered unspoken as I toiled to prove my worth, striving to be seen in the spaces you had yet to create. I yearned for a room to share my true self, to express myself like any child should, but those spaces were rare.

You never saw me – not the entirety of me. Only in moments labeled as "negative" did your gaze find mine. I comprehend now, uncle; your battles, internal and external, formed an armor against feelings, against the present moment. Physically there, but never wholly present. But uncle, the wounds you carried then became the source of my pain. I was a child, defenseless, lacking the choice to escape or the understanding to comprehend. You unwittingly shaped my thoughts, my behaviors, and my reality. The programming you offered was a mixed bag – a journey to where I stand today—grateful for the lessons and values, yet grappling with remnants of the struggles. Uncle, you possessed the ability to reflect on and question your thoughts, patterns, and behavior, to overcome the anger and fear within you that you projected out into your outer world.

Uncle, forgiveness is now the thread that weaves through our shared story. I understand it wasn't your duty to love me; that was mine. A lesson in self-love, although life might have unfolded differently if love flowed more freely. I love you, uncle, unconditionally. May you, too, find the path to self-love and release any lingering guilt or pain.

All is forgiven, and nothing lingers to forgive any longer.

My cries to my aunt:

Do you love me, Tia? Can you see me in the fragments of my past, feel the echoes of my pain? Sometimes, it feels like you do love me, but the words remain unspoken, perhaps lost in the void of self-love you struggled to find. Your heart, heavy with anger, scared me. I knew it was not directed at me, yet the violence you wielded in disciplining Aria, my sister at heart, pierced my soul. She is my best friend, and watching her suffer hurt me too.

Tia, your life was marked by trauma – a mother's departure in infancy, a void that echoed through your years. You saw a reflection of me in yourself, and in your compassion, I felt a glimpse of the love you struggled to express. Your happiness was my goal; I yearned to see that version of you every day. Yet, I sensed your pain, a burden you carried. In my attempts to alleviate it, I offered massages, cooked dinners, and cleaned the house – anything to stave off your anger or sadness. You were a different person when joy colored your days. I craved that happiness for you, even though you held so much grief inside. Unprocessed emotions, a silent storm within, left you grappling in the absence of guidance. But, Tia, you held the power to heal – within yourself. Feeling, crying, releasing – the path to your own solace. It was time to question behaviors and patterns, a journey that required a pause. I understand, Tia, that the time wasn't right for you then. Yet, in the depths of your struggles, I want you to know that my love remains unconditional—grateful for taking me in, for raising me in the best way you knew how.

My inner child cries to my mother:

Mama, I'm scared. In this new land, surrounded by family I barely know, the language feels strange and unfamiliar. I ache for you, Mama, for your love and comforting presence. I yearn for the warmth of your hugs and the solace of your embrace. The pain and fear are overwhelming. Nights are filled with tears as I think of you and everyone back home. Why did you let this happen, Mama? Did you stop loving me?

Now, Mama, I understand. Your love was unwavering, and your intentions were noble. You sought a better life for me, unaware of the costs. The pain I would endure, the despair that would grip my heart – how could you have known? You hadn't walked that path. Anger lingered in my heart for so long, but I'm sorry, Mama. I comprehend now that you, too, had your battles and traumas—a young mother facing the world, steering uncharted territories. All is forgiven, Mama, for there is nothing to forgive. I love you unconditionally. My heart, though heavy, carries the understanding that you did what you thought was best for us.

Chapter 4: Moving to Canada

In 1992, after waiting a little over two years, my Canadian PR was finally approved. I was just a nine-and-a-half-year-old kid, but the news of reuniting with my dad in Vancouver, BC, filled my heart with joy. Those initial weeks in Canada were like a dream come true, a respite from the struggles that I have faced. Finally, I got to experience the warmth of a loving family.

In the beginning, my dad made an effort to be present and spend time with me to bridge the gap created by years of separation. It was a welcome change from the past. My stepmother, during those first few weeks, radiated kindness and consideration. She went the extra mile to make my room feel like home. She even got me some new clothes, making me feel special. The warmth and excitement she showed in having me around were like a comforting embrace, lifting my spirits. The walls echoed with laughter, and the air carried the scent of newfound familial joy.

However, little did I know that this idyllic beginning would soon face its own set of challenges, unraveling the delicate fabric of familial bliss that I cherished. Soon, it was revealed to me that this newfound sense of family bliss was short-lived. The warmth dwindled a few months after my arrival, replaced by an unforeseen coldness. It seemed apparent that being a stepmother was a challenge she hadn't fully anticipated.

I found myself resenting the new clothes she chose for me. The new clothes she enthusiastically provided, in hindsight, seemed to be more of a torment than a blessing. I can't determine if it was intentional or simply a matter of questionable taste, but those clothes became a source of ridicule at school. The taunts and laughter of classmates echoed daily in the hallways. Thanks to the clothes she bought for me, I became the target of mockery due to my wardrobe.

The situation worsened as she asserted more control, and her attempt to contribute to my appearance took a distressing turn. My once-long hair was chopped short, rendering me with a boyish look that persisted for the next few years. Each day at school became a battleground, a struggle to endure the laughter and mockery. There were a few of my friends, some compassionate souls, who felt a sense of pity for me. And during those challenging circumstances, a truly remarkable friend entered my life.

She happened to be an aspiring actress. Her kindness became a guiding light in the darkness I was experiencing. Every day, she would go out of her way to bring me a change of clothes, a simple yet profound gesture that provided a much-needed semblance of normalcy in the overwhelming sea of humiliation I was going through.

Her actions went beyond the physical gift of clothes; they extended to the emotional realm, mending the fragments of my shattered self-esteem. Through her compassion, I began to feel seen again, as if she had unearthed a connection with my classmates that had eluded me for far too long. Her genuine care created a bridge, allowing me to rebuild a sense of belonging that had been fractured by adversity. In her aspiring actress spirit, she played a starring role in restoring not only my wardrobe but also my confidence and connection with others. I must say that thanks to her, I began to feel seen again, finding a connection with my classmates that had eluded me for so long.

I lived with my stepbrother under the same roof. He radiated youthful energy, though his occasional bouts of annoyance were hard to overlook. While we attended different schools, our paths intersected at the same after-school program. One day, his observant eyes caught the subtle shift in my attire – a detail that soon birthed a daily ordeal in my not-so-peaceful life.

In an act of sibling innocence, my stepbrother discovered I wasn't wearing the same clothes and shoes from home. He promptly informed his mother about my wardrobe alterations, alleging that I had changed into someone else's clothing and shoes at school. This triggered a distressing routine.

After that, each morning, under the watchful eyes of my stepmother, my bags underwent meticulous inspection. But it didn't end there—she would thoroughly check me, taking away any bit of privacy I had. The fear of being accused of wearing someone else's clothes became a daily worry. The clothes I borrowed, usually kept in the after-school program, became a hidden secret, away from curious looks.

Each day felt like walking on a tightrope, trying to have a normal childhood while dealing with the constant scrutiny that could easily disrupt any sense of stability. It was a tricky balance between wanting things to be normal and the constant fear of everything falling apart.

Amidst the challenging dynamics of my home life, there was a beacon of light at the daycare center — a remarkable teacher named Marissa. Her presence was a solace, a refuge from the storm that brewed within the confines of my family. It wasn't just a teacher-student relationship; it felt like she saw through the layers of my struggles, offering a genuine connection that transcended the boundaries of the classroom.

Marissa wasn't just an observer; she was an active participant in my life, a silent ally against the adversity I faced at home. She bore witness to the mistreatment and the emotional scars that were inflicted daily, and she decided to be a force of positivity in my world. The indifference she displayed toward my stepmother and dad hinted at an unwavering focus on the well-being of the child standing before her.

Her acts of kindness were profound and consistent. Marissa went above and beyond her role, creating a safe haven within the daycare's nurturing environment. In those moments, I felt more than just seen; I felt loved, appreciated, and valued. It was a reprieve from the ceaseless scrutiny and judgment that awaited me at home.

The impact Marissa had on my life lingered long after those tumultuous days. I often find myself reminiscing about her, reflecting on the profound difference she made in my life. The desire to reconnect with her, to express gratitude for being that unwavering pillar of support, lingers in my thoughts.

In this story of life, Marissa's role was essential — a guardian angel whose influence shaped the resilience that would carry me through the storms that lay ahead. If this book happens to find its way to her, I hope she recognizes the lasting impression she left and reaches out to me one day, completing a circle of gratitude and acknowledgment.

Continuing my story, one day, I brought my friend's shoes home with me by mistake. They were inside my bag.

"Shit! How am I supposed to sneak these shoes out of the house?" I mumbled to myself.

In desperation to avoid the storm, I jogged my brain and came up with a plan. I decided to wear a dress with two pockets and craftily stashed one shoe in each pocket of the dress. With my jacket concealing my ingenious strategy, I approached my stepmother for the routine morning inspection. After enduring months of intrusive strip searches, she had shifted to a seemingly less invasive pat-down from head to toe.

As her hands moved over my clothing, a surge of anxiety gripped me. During this pat-down, the inevitable happened – one of the shoes tumbled to the ground. I remember the sudden surge of anxiety as her gaze fixated on the fallen shoe. Swiftly, she picked it up, and a storm of anger erupted.

The shoe, once a simple part of my fashion escape, transformed into a weapon of punishment. It became a relentless tool, striking my head and face with each hurl of insults.

"You ungrateful bitch!" she shouted as she whacked my face with the shoe.

The room echoed with her hurtful words, labeling me as an ungrateful person. The weight of that moment lingered, leaving me not just physically bruised but emotionally battered by the harsh torrent of anger and insults. This incident wasn't a one-time thing; it was part of an ongoing pattern of both physical and verbal abuse. There were numerous instances where her anger erupted into slaps and harsh words, particularly when my dad wasn't present. Confrontation only prompted her to deny everything, using denial as a shield to hide the scars she caused. Whenever my dad questioned her, she bluntly denied the accusations, portraying me as a liar and a bad person.

Scratch marks from her aggressive outbursts adorned my face, serving as silent witnesses to the brutality I endured. These marks were concealed beneath the façade of normalcy whenever I stepped outside my home. The contrast between the public perception and the hidden reality created a disheartening duality, where the pain and suffering remained veiled, overshadowed by the pretense of an ordinary existence.

These relentless incidents etched a profound and lasting imprint on the canvas of my mind and soul. As a mere 10 to 11 years old, I found myself grappling with the weight of my experiences, seeking solace in the only way my young mind could comprehend.

It began with the desperate expression of a desire to escape, manifested in letters fraught with the yearning to run away from the torment that had become my daily existence. However, the desperation within me evolved, deepening its roots, and gradually, these letters transformed into haunting echoes of a much darker sentiment – the contemplation of ending my own life. The weight of the preceding five years, since the tender age of seven, had been a burden too heavy for a young soul to bear. Yet, there was a flicker of light within, an ember that refused to be extinguished. It may have been the lingering presence of my grandmother, a silent companion through all the hardships. I was lucky that I had a few people backing me up in my troubled preteen days. Those people showered me with their love and kindness. Marissa, my daycare teacher, stood as one of these pillars, and another crucial figure was my counselor and sports coach, Steven. His influence on my life during this delicate period was immeasurable.

In 6th grade, Steven attempted to convince my dad and stepmother to let me join the volleyball and basketball teams, endeavors I had a true passion for and in which I excelled. Despite my evident talent, my family opposed the idea. Undeterred, Steven became a source of solace and encouragement, pulling me out of class for training sessions and heartfelt conversations about life and aspirations. He saw beyond the challenges I faced at home and became the source of love and peace I desperately needed – my earthly guardian, much like Marissa.

It wasn't until grade 7 that my dad, at last, relented, allowing me to participate in sports despite my stepmother's objections. I eagerly joined the school team, and almost instantly, my skills garnered attention, leading to an invitation to play for a club volleyball team. This opportunity, facilitated by Steven's unwavering support, became a turning point, a glimmer of hope in the midst of my tumultuous adolescence.

Obviously, neither my dad nor my stepmother gave their approval or showed any willingness to bear the financial responsibility for my sports training. Despite my passion and dedication, the support I sought from them remained elusive, adding an extra layer of challenge to my pursuit of athletic endeavors. In the face of disapproval and financial reluctance from both my dad and stepmother, Steve became my advocate. Recognizing my athletic potential, he stepped forward to champion my cause. The principal, deeply impressed by my skills, took it a step further by generously covering the costs of my training. Their support not only fueled my passion for sports but also served as a powerful testament to the impact of genuine advocacy and belief in one's potential.

Remarkably, my parents never attended any of my games, seemingly indifferent to my burgeoning talents. However, in a surprising twist of events, a pivotal moment arrived when, out of the blue, my dad made an unexpected appearance at one of my basketball games. The atmosphere crackled with nerves and anticipation as I played, knowing that, for the first time, my father was watching me in the audience.

As the game progressed, the principal, clearly impressed by my performance, took the initiative to approach my father. His words of admiration echoed through the gym, emphasizing that he hadn't witnessed such a combination of strength and skill in a player for a long time. It was a powerful moment that seemed to break through the barriers that had kept my dad at a distance from my sporting journey.

For the first time in a while, I felt a surge of emotions – a blend of hope, validation, and a touch of vulnerability. It was as if a spotlight had been cast on the dedication I poured into my passion, and my father, in that moment, saw beyond our complex family dynamics. It was a moment that seemingly broke through the barriers, allowing my dad to see me with fresh eyes – a poignant instance of recognition after a prolonged period of being unseen. The basketball court became a stage where my efforts were not only seen but celebrated, fostering a newfound connection between us that transcended the boundaries of our challenging past.

A few months passed by, marked by the intensification of verbal and emotional abuse. During that time, a significant shift occurred when, at the age of 12, my father, sensing the need for change, finally allowed me to grow my hair once again. This seemingly small concession proved to be a turning point, empowering me to gather the courage to open up to my father about the profound unhappiness that had taken root within me.

As I shared the relentless mistreatment endured by my stepmother in his absence, something shifted. This time, my father not only listened but, to my surprise, expressed belief in my words. He revealed that he had always sensed the toxicity but clung to the ideal of a unified family, which he now recognized as an unsustainable facade.

This acknowledgment marked a crucial moment, breaking through the walls of denial and setting the stage for a deeper understanding between us. It was a moment of truth that laid the foundation for confronting the harsh realities within our home and, perhaps, the possibility of forging a healthier path forward.

Despite my father's sincere attempt to play the role of a father and maintain the semblance of a united family, the weight of his own struggles proved too burdensome. His addiction habits and a set of misplaced priorities often overshadowed the potential for sound decision-making in my best interest. Instead of providing stability, his presence was marked by an incessant pursuit of parties and substances, further deepening the chasm within our family. Within the toxic dynamics of our household, I found myself caught in the crossfire of domestic violence. The once sporadic instances of verbal and emotional abuse escalated into a disheartening routine, with both my father and stepmother engaging in heated arguments and, at times, violent confrontations. The echoes of yelling became the dissonant soundtrack of our household, creating an environment where peace seemed like a distant memory.

While grappling with the suffocating environment of our house, another storm struck us. One day, police came to our doorstep and took away my father. That night, he was arrested, casting a chilling shadow over our already fractured household. As a child wrestling with the confusion of the situation, I couldn't fathom why my father, seemingly defending himself from my stepmother's aggression, was the one taken away. Witnessing the altercation left me with fear and bewilderment. I had naively believed that defending oneself was a right, but this incident shattered that perception.

Alone in my room that night, anxiety gripped me. The fear of the unknown consumed my thoughts, creating a sense of vulnerability that lingered in the air. Questions raced through my mind like a relentless storm – would I be expelled from the house, left to wander the streets as a homeless child? Or, perhaps even more terrifying, would my stepmother unleash her anger on me next, subjecting me to a fate worse than I could fathom? The darkness seemed to amplify my solitude, and I lay in bed, yearning for an escape from the haunting uncertainties that loomed over me. Sleep eluded me as every creak in the house and every distant sound intensified my apprehension. The night passed like a silent symphony of dread, with the possibility of something dreadful lurking around every corner. It was a harrowing experience, leaving an indelible mark on my young soul. My father was released the next day, and he came to take me with him, ushering me into a world of paradoxes. Instead of a comforting refuge, we found ourselves at his friend's house, surrounded by an atmosphere of alcohol and drug-induced euphoria. Laughter echoed through the air as my father and his buddies reveled in the haze of intoxication, oblivious to the turmoil that had recently shaken our lives.

In the midst of their merriment, I grappled with confusion and disbelief. How could he simply cast aside the gravity of the recent events? This internal confusion, however, found resolution as I began to understand that, for my father, this was an escape—an attempt to distance himself from the harsh reality that threatened to consume him. The camaraderie, the laughter, and the alcohol offered a fleeting reprieve, a momentary distraction from the complexities of his existence.

As I observed this spectacle, my heart yearned for clarity, for a sense of normalcy that seemed elusive. The profound realization, born from years of resentment and misunderstanding, eventually dawned upon me: neither my father nor my stepmother were solely architects of their actions. Instead, their behaviors were the manifested consequences of unhealed traumas, a poignant reminder that compassion often resides in understanding the roots of one's struggles.

In the midst of the chaos, I yearned for a semblance of understanding, a bridge that could span the chasm of our fractured family dynamics. This epiphany softened the edges of my resentment, fostering a budding empathy for the pain that shaped their actions. It was a complex realization, urging me to navigate the balance between self-preservation and extending compassion to those who had caused me so much anguish. The journey toward healing involved acknowledging the wounds inflicted upon me and recognizing the unresolved pain that fueled their actions.

Looking into the web of human behavior, I've come to realize that understanding the motivations behind actions is a far more potent force than the condemnation of those actions. In the pursuit of healing, I've adopted a lens of comprehension, choosing to disentangle the threads of circumstances that shaped my father and stepmother's behaviors. This paradigm shift from judgment to understanding has become the compass guiding my journey toward forgiveness.

The key to unlocking the shackles of the past is forgiveness. It's not merely an act of absolving others for their transgressions; it's a profound liberation of the self. The journey of forgiveness is an arduous yet transformative process that involves acknowledging the pain and embracing the power to let go. It's a cathartic dance between the past and the present, a therapeutic unraveling of the knots that bound the heart.

Yet, as I pen down these words, the pain resurfaces. The wounds, though healing, carry the weight of the past, and every stroke of the pen feels like a step back in time. The raw emotion, the palpable hurt, and the vivid recollections make it an immersive experience—an unintended journey back to moments etched in the corridors of my memory. Each word is a confrontation with the ghosts of the past, with the echoes of pain that refuse to fade away. This book becomes a mirror reflecting the visceral intensity of lived experiences, evoking sensations as if I'm reliving those moments once more.

Chapter 5: New York

The spring of 1995 marked my return to New York, stepping into the familiar territory of my uncle's home. The reason behind this move was the dissolution of my father's marriage to my stepmother. In a heart-to-heart conversation, my dad shared that he lacked the confidence and meant to single-handedly raise me, leading to the decision to grant custody to my uncle.

As I set foot in New York for the second time, a flood of emotions swirled within me. Excitement and happiness welled up, fueled by the prospect of sharing my joys and sorrows with my cousin Aria, a companion in the journey of life. The anticipation of a new adventure tinged the air, blending with the familiarity of my uncle's household.

The warmth of family and the promise of a supportive environment served as beacons guiding me through the upcoming journey. Aria, my cousin, emerged as my confidante, a person with whom I could openly share both the highs and lows of life. The familiarity of family and the sense of belonging offered a comforting assurance, a stark contrast to the uncertainties that had characterized my life before.

Entering this new chapter, I carried with me the resilience forged through earlier trials. While the echoes of the past lingered, there was a glimmer of hope that this phase would provide the stability and understanding I yearned for.

Life in New York took on a different rhythm as I settled into my uncle's home. During the day, my uncle attended to the responsibilities of the store and restaurant. In the evening, he worked his shift at IBM. He owned a modest restaurant and convenience store nestled in one of the toughest areas of Newburgh. Our living quarters were perched above the convenience store, a snug two-bedroom apartment where I spent my days. Sharing a room with my three cousins became the norm, and surprisingly, I found peace in the close quarters. The limited space didn't bother me because the bond I shared with my cousins eclipsed any need for personal space. There was a unique joy in facing the challenges of a small living area together, laughter echoing through the shared space, and the warmth of familial connection enveloping us.

Our apartment became a microcosm of love and togetherness, a sanctuary amidst the tumult of the surrounding neighborhood. I cherished the company, the late-night conversations, and the shared dreams that filled our room. It was in those close quarters that I discovered the resilience of family bonds – a warmth of support, understanding, and love.

The convenience store downstairs hummed with life, a testament to my uncle's hard work and determination. The aroma of freshly prepared meals wafted through the air, mingling with the lively chatter of customers. The store was more than a business; it was a hub of community interaction, a place where stories echoed, and connections were forged.

In the heart of one of Newburgh's toughest neighborhoods, we navigated life together, finding strength in unity and comfort in shared experiences.

My love for my cousins deepened, and the challenges of our environment only served to reinforce the bonds that held us together. As my hair grew and my youthful spirit blossomed, life in New York brought new experiences. At the age of 12, I found myself attending a new junior high school during the day and lending a hand in the family store afterward. Little did I know my journey in this small town would bring attention I had never experienced back in Canada. The days at school introduced me to a new path of learning and social interaction. My age seemed to defy my appearance; I looked older than my 12 years.

The newfound attention wasn't limited to the classroom; it spilled into the family's convenience store. Male customers would offer glances that lingered a bit too long, and at school, I became the exotic newcomer, capturing the interest of older boys.

These shifts in attention stirred strange emotions within me. The novelty of being noticed sparked both curiosity and unease. I grappled with the unfamiliar dynamics of attraction and the awareness that I was now seen through different eyes. The attention became a nuanced layer in my adolescent journey, an unexpected facet of growing up in a new environment.

Navigating this newfound visibility was both thrilling and challenging. The echoes of my past mingled with the present, creating experiences that shaped my understanding of relationships and self-image. In the midst of school assignments, store responsibilities, and the complexities of teenage emotions, I found myself caught in a delicate dance of self-discovery in the vibrant backdrop of Newburgh, NY. I was frequently told I appeared older than 12 and a half years of age, a sentiment I internalized. I felt I had to mature faster than most 12-year-olds. Unfortunately, my upbringing deviated from the norms of a healthy childhood.

The attention, both in school and at the family store, created a sense of novelty that I hadn't encountered before. In this uncharted territory, Aria, my ever-supportive cousin, became my guide. Aria wasn't just a cousin; she was a true sister and a vital companion in this journey. Wherever she ventured, I followed, finding solace in her company. Aria's inclusive nature ensured I wasn't just a newcomer; I was an integral part of her social circle. During those moments when it was just Aria and me, our living room transformed into a haven of joy. Dancing became our weekly ritual, a safe haven where we could lose ourselves in the rhythm of music. The beats of "I Like to Move It Move It," the soulful notes of "Candy Rain," and every melody from Selena became the soundtrack of our shared moments. Aria, with her infectious energy, taught me the art of dance, and through these lively sessions, our bond deepened, blanketing the challenges of living in a new town.

That night, Aria and I ventured out to a friend's house, embracing the thrill of teenage rebellion. Our curfew loomed over us, a strict deadline to be back home by 9 p.m. However, caught up in the moment, I became the catalyst for breaking our agreed-upon curfew. Aria, responsible and mindful of our commitment, repeatedly urged us to return back and adhere to the curfew. The weight of guilt settled on me, an overwhelming sense that the deviation from the plan was entirely my doing. As the night passed, the clash between the desire to extend our time and the responsibility of keeping to the curfew intensified, leaving me grappling with the consequences of my choices.

Anyways, after partying to our hearts' content, we arrived

home well past 11 p.m. The house was cloaked in darkness, and the quiet streets held an air of reprimand for our tardiness. In the absence of cell phones in 1995, Aria attempted to use the landline, but our efforts to communicate our delayed return were met with unanswered calls. As we parked in front of the house, an ominous sight awaited us. My aunt, a silhouette against the dimly lit doorway, stood waiting. The expression etched across her face was unmistakable—an amalgamation of concern, frustration, and anger. The palpable tension hung in the air, an unspoken consequence of breaking the curfew and returning home late. I could feel the weight of her disapproval even before she uttered a word.

The atmosphere inside the house grew heavy as soon as the front door closed behind us. My aunt's frustration manifested instantly, and without a moment's hesitation, she seized a fistful of Aria's hair, wrapping it around her wrist like a vise. The forceful yank pulled Aria up the stairs, the echo of her stifled cries ringing in my ears.

Haunted by guilt and fear, I walked up the staircase at a sluggish pace, each step marked by the weight of responsibility for the transgression. My presence seemed invisible to my aunt, as if I were a mere specter haunting the periphery of that scene.

Upon reaching the top of the stairs, the brutal reality unfolded before me. My aunt, fueled by anger and disappointment, subjected Aria to a merciless beating. The sounds of each blow, the cries of pain, and the sight of Aria's vulnerability left me feeling nauseous and engulfed in self-disgust. It was an internal battle, wrestling with the idea that this was my fault, an irrational tendency ingrained by the complexities of trauma.

In those harrowing moments, the dynamics of blame and responsibility became entangled, a testament to the ways in which trauma can warp one's perception of culpability. The echoes of that night would reverberate through the corridors of memory, a haunting reminder of the weight we carry, even when the burden is not truly ours to bear. That night taught me a crucial lesson, imprinting it into the depths of my subconscious – the notion that invisibility and silence could serve as an impenetrable shield, protecting me from the storms of chaos that brewed within the walls of our small apartment. It had been years since the last time I bore witness to such a brutal scene, and the haunting question persisted: Why did I remain silent? Why did I allow my cousin to shoulder the blame alone?

As I reflect on those years, the answer becomes clear – fear. Fear, a paralyzing force that held me captive, was rooted in the traumatic experiences that had left me feeling rejected and unwanted before. The prospect of opening my mouth and raising my voice was an unbearable risk, one that threatened the fragile stability I had managed to carve out in my newfound home.

In the shadows of that night, I grappled with the complexities of survival, a silent observer of the violence inflicted upon my cousin. The weight of unspoken words pressed heavily on my chest as I struggled to reconcile the guilt of my silence with the fear of becoming a target myself. Little did I know, this was a survival strategy I had unwittingly adopted – the art of blending into the background, avoiding the crossfire of anger and retribution.

The echoes of that night would resonate through the years, a painful reminder of the silent complicity I carried. It was a lesson borne out of necessity, a survival instinct forged in the crucible of trauma.

As the days passed in the routine of the small store, a new character stepped into my life – Felix, a charming presence that disrupted the ordinary cadence of my teenage life. One day, Felix strolled into the store, his introduction carrying an air of confident familiarity.

"Hello," he greeted with a warmth that transcended the simplicity of the words. "I'm Felix, and you are gorgeous. I live just across the street with my family, so I'll be seeing you around more often," he added, his words hanging in the air boldly.

In the ensuing weeks, Felix's daily visits to the store became a fixture, a routine that blurred the lines between casual encounters and deliberate crossings of paths. I discovered that he was 19 years old, living with his girlfriend just across the street. Yet, unfazed by the fact that he lived with his girlfriend and that I was a 12.5-year-old child, he indulged in what seemed to be a playful flirtation, but in reality, I was being groomed. His consistent presence painted the mundane walls of the store with a palette of emotions, and I found myself caught between shyness and attraction.

The store, with its unassuming exterior, hid a secret – a door near the cashier area that led to the upstairs apartment. As Felix continued his daily visits, that door became a threshold to a world of unspoken possibilities. Each encounter left a trace of anticipation, an unspoken question that lingered in the air.

I never imagined that these seemingly innocent interactions would unfurl into a series of events that would alter the course of my adolescence. On an ordinary afternoon during my shift at the store, something changed. As I meandered toward the door leading to the upstairs apartment, I sensed Felix's presence trailing closely behind me. Casting a glance over my shoulder, I noticed Felix silently shadowing my steps, his presence lingering in the quiet transition between the store and the hidden chambers above.

"Why are you following me?" I turned and questioned him with a curious edge in my voice.

His response, delivered with a peculiar sincerity and desire, hung in the air.

"I've been dying to kiss you," he confessed, the words weaving a subtle tension into the atmosphere.

I found myself in a state of utter disbelief as Felix's words were accompanied by his forceful actions, pulling me toward the wall and pressing his lips against my neck. The suddenness of it all left me reeling, my mind struggling to process the rapid escalation of the situation. I felt a sense of paralysis wash over me, unable to fully comprehend or react to the overwhelming onslaught of his advances. My thoughts were a jumble of confusion, my emotions a chaotic mix of fear and uncertainty.

As his lips trailed toward my mouth, a sense of unease settled deep within me. I wasn't sure how to respond, my body tense and rigid as I grappled with the onslaught of conflicting emotions. The feeling of helplessness was suffocating, as if I were suspended in a nightmarish limbo, unable to break free from his unwelcome grasp.

The situation took a harrowing turn as Felix's hands began to roam, exploring every inch of my body with a disturbing sense of entitlement. I felt a sickening knot form in the pit of my stomach as his touch ventured toward my most intimate areas. His hands, with a chilling sense of violation, made their way down to my genitals, rubbing and touching me through my clothing. The sensation was repulsive, and I was overwhelmed with a profound sense of vulnerability and shame.

Time seemed to stand still as the groping continued, each moment stretching into an eternity of discomfort and distress. I was frozen in place, unable to find the strength to push him away or speak out against the violation I was experiencing. The weight of my silence felt crushing, yet I couldn't bring myself to fight back. I simply allowed this distressing encounter to unfold; my mind clouded with emotions that would haunt me long after the physical contact ended.

In that suspended instant, frozen by the complexity of uncertain feelings, I grappled with an inner landscape in flux. The store, once a backdrop to daily routines, transformed into an arena where unspoken desires and hesitant vulnerabilities converged.

For years, I carried the weight of self-blame, shouldering the burden of responsibility for the distressing encounter. I chastised myself, convincing my mind that I had somehow allowed and even desired the violation that had unfolded. But how could a 12-year-old possibly comprehend or willingly seek out such a harrowing experience?

His words echoed in my mind, haunting me with their sinister implications.

"I have been dying to kiss you for weeks. You will be mine."

The chilling declaration reverberated through my being, leaving me feeling trapped and powerless in the face of his predatory intentions.

After he finally departed, I retreated upstairs, seeking solace in the quiet confines of my thoughts. Alone with my emotions, I grappled with the bewildering aftermath of what had just transpired. It felt as if the very fabric of my existence had been irrevocably altered as if a piece of my innocence had been callously stolen away.

In the wake of that distressing encounter, a profound shift occurred within me. It was as though a relentless hunger for attention and physical contact had taken root, driving me to seek out more of the same. Yet, in the depths of my soul, I recognized that the true yearning lay far beyond the physical realm. What I craved, more than anything, was to be truly seen and loved, to forge genuine connections that would fill the void within me.

In my desperate pursuit of love and connection, I unwittingly sacrificed my own well-being, offering up my body in exchange for fleeting moments of validation and affection. The realization pierced through me like a jagged shard of glass, leaving me raw and vulnerable in its wake.

The truth of the matter settled heavily upon my heart, a burden too weighty to bear. I grappled with the agonizing understanding that Felix, along with all the other men who had exploited my vulnerability, had callously robbed me of my childhood. Their actions had irreversibly shattered the innocence and purity that should have defined those formative years, leaving behind a trail of scars that would linger for a lifetime.

Studies suggest that the repercussions of childhood sexual abuse can be severe, leading to an increased risk of over-sexualized behavior in my case. It's a harsh reality that I've had to confront, but I know that I'm not alone in experiencing it. As a child, I lacked the language or understanding to express the complex emotions I was feeling. What I did know was that I longed for love, connection, and a sense of belonging that was sorely lacking in my life.

Looking back, it's evident that my family and those closest to me failed to meet my emotional needs. The attention and affection that should have been freely given were noticeably absent. Instead, I was left to navigate the confusing and overwhelming feelings that came with being sexually abused as a child. It's a burden that no one should have to bear, yet it's one that far too many of us carry.

Despite the pain and trauma that I've endured, I refuse to let it define me. I'm committed to healing and finding a way to move forward. It's not easy, but I'm taking it one day at a time. With the support of loved ones and a strong sense of resilience, I know that I can overcome the scars of my past and build a brighter future.

During the following weeks, Felix made a habit of stopping by the store every day. Each time, he would take my hand and lead me to the same hallway area that led upstairs, where he would corner me against the wall. He always insisted that I keep it a secret. By then, I found myself reciprocating his kisses. He would dry hump me, the friction of his body against mine leaving no doubt about his intentions. Dry sex was occurring, and he also expressed a strong desire to engage in penetrative sex with me right there and then. The confusion and fear I felt were overwhelming as I struggled to justify his behavior.

I desired more attention, and it came effortlessly from the men around me. Felix started bringing his 23-year-old cousin, Jonathan, to the store, and Jonathan wasted no time grooming me. One day after school, I spotted Jonathan by his car with some friends. He called me over, and as I approached, he embraced me. Then, as I tried to pull away, he held my hands and drew me closer, locking eyes with me. Before I knew it, we were kissing.

Jonathan became a consistent presence in my life, picking me up from school week after week. Our encounters would often escalate to intense make-out sessions in the back of his car. Though we never went all the way, the boundaries we pushed were undeniable. His hands explored every inch of my body, leaving me feeling violated. It became evident that penetration was not necessary for the damage to take its toll.

In an attempt to cope, I sought solace in the attention of older boys from school and men. I allowed them to take advantage of my vulnerability, though I kept a firm limit on how far I would let them go. It was a twisted cycle, a bittersweet escape from the pain I carried within me for far too long.

Unconsciously, I was becoming addicted to this type of attention and to the feeling of being desired. Paradoxically, I felt empowered, yet deep down, I may have been attempting to undo the sexual abuse and reclaim control by "allowing" these men to exploit me, in hopes of a different outcome. Keeping firm limits was my way of "controlling" the situation. But the reality was, I was spiraling out of control.

Unbeknownst to me, exposing my struggles to the open air would prove to be a transformative experience. It was as if ripping off a bandage and confronting the wound directly offered the most effective treatment for the tender and raw emotions I had carried with me for what felt like an eternity. The anger and pain that had consumed me began to manifest outwardly. I became an easily triggered individual, unleashing my fury on anyone that I perceived as a threat or judgmental.

My teachers bore the brunt of my unleashed wrath, as I lashed out with curses and misplaced aggression whenever I felt judged. I refused to remain silent when I believed I was being attacked or disrespected. This newfound anger spilled over into physical altercations with other female students as I let my pain dictate my actions.

Though the journey was tumultuous, it was in confronting the depths of my pain that I was able to slowly heal. The path toward redemption was a difficult one, but it was a necessary step toward reclaiming my sense of self-worth and finding solace amidst the chaos that once defined my existence.

During that turbulent period, it felt like I was spiraling out of control. Suspension notices seemed to arrive in my mailbox every other week as if they were timed perfectly to erode what little self-esteem I had left. The whispers and rumors that circulated around town painted me as a stuck-up bitch and a promiscuous temptress, fueled by my interactions with men and the attention I garnered from the male gaze.

The town, a repository of whispered judgments, began crafting a narrative that cast me as a wayward figure – a "bad woman" whose reputation was entangled in the complexities of rumors. The whispers, like echoes in the wind, reached every corner of the community, attributing my perceived missteps to entanglements with men. It's interesting how I was perceived as a "woman" and not a child or teenager. I found myself being shamed instead of the men who exploited me. Rather than receiving support or guidance, I faced criticism, even from my own family. Sadly, I was viewed as a disgrace and disappointment to them, rather than someone in desperate need of assistance. How could they have recognized the signs of sexual abuse when they were also victims of their own upbringing? Their focus was solely on external perceptions and how my behavior affected their reputation. The male gaze, a relentless companion, became the harbinger of judgment, shaping the narrative of my adolescence. The weight of these rumors bore down on me, a heavy realization of the multifaceted abuse that had woven its threads through my childhood and teenage years.

The pain of recognition cut deep, the wounds of the past surfacing with poignant clarity. Amidst the ache, a profound need emerged – the need for connection with my higher self, a desire for my inner child and inner teenager to find expression and release. The journey inward beckoned a call to meditation, a sanctuary where emotions, expressions, and the unspoken words of my younger self could find solace and resonance. The quest for healing continued an intimate dialogue between past and present, a yearning to assure my inner child that safety had finally become a reality.

In the sacred realm of meditation, I started a journey, an ethereal bridge between my present self and the echoes of my inner child and teenager. The whispers from the depths of my soul resonated, seeking connection, expression, and a shared understanding with my father. The silent conversation revealed a plea for healing and reconciliation.

The Whispers of My Inner Child, Higher Self, and Teen Self to My Dad:

Dad, as I reflect on our shared history, a wish lingers in my heart for a past adorned with beautiful memories steeped in love and connection. Despite the complexities, I wouldn't trade the precious moments we did share for anything in this world. I acknowledge the depth of your journey, the traumas that shaped you, and the patterns that conditioned your expressions. I understand, Dad, that the substances you took were your escape from confronting the demons that lurked within. The absence of a male figure in your life left you navigating uncharted territories, unaware of how to embody that role. Yet, Dad, the unhealed facets of your being cast shadows on my own path, leaving me without the presence of a nurturing father figure.

This absence, Dad, cultivated a void that echoed throughout my life, sparking a relentless need for male attention and validation. The pursuit of the masculine gaze became a constant companion, steering me toward a quest for acceptance. This void, this yearning, became a thread woven into the fabric of my existence, paving the way for the challenges that lay ahead.

Dad, I forgive you – as a child and as a woman. I release the burden of abandonment, the ache of your intermittent presence, the echoes of anger, and the scars of emotional, verbal, and physical wounds. Our journey was shaped by your pain, and I extend forgiveness, understanding that there is nothing to truly forgive. Please, don't carry the weight of blame, for you were navigating your own storm, taught to embody a toughness that belied the vulnerability within.

Dad, the notion of expressing emotions wasn't something you believed men should do. You were molded to suppress your feelings because, in your eyes, allowing vulnerability would bring societal shame, a blow to the ego hard to bear. Dad, I want you to know that I release you from any inner sorrow or guilt that may linger. I comprehend that you carried deeper wounds than I could perceive.

Your actions were a product of your conditioning, a reflection of your own understanding. I forgive you, not because there was ever any fault in me, but because I've chosen the healing path. I've come to realize that clinging to anger and resentment only inflicts more pain, while love holds the power to heal. I don't blame you anymore because, in my understanding now, there was never truly anything to blame or forgive. Your manifestations in the world mirror how you perceive yourself.

Chapter 6: Meeting My Karmic Partner

At the tender age of thirteen or perhaps fourteen, I was hit with a jarring realization that I was still undocumented. This was a real shock to me, triggered by a simple desire to work at McDonald's to earn and buy things for myself. I just wanted to be free from dependency and do something on my own. Despite the valiant efforts of my aunt and uncle to provide for me, financial limitations were an undeniable reality. It became apparent that my uncle was losing the convenience store and restaurant. I believe this realization was hard for him to come to terms with. He juggled two roles, working at the convenience store and his regular evening job at IBM.

My aunt toiled away at a light bulb factory, and our budget was tight. We were fortunate to receive only three to five outfits per year, or at best, until the arrival of Christmas. Consequently, my cousin Aria and I had to share clothing, and we became experts at creating a diverse range of outfits from our compact closet. The process of conjuring up fancy dresses from our limited wardrobe was mentally taxing, and we exhausted all our creative faculties.

The struggle to make ends meet was real, and the limitations of our resources shaped our approach to clothing and personal possessions. Yet, in the midst of financial constraints, a spirit of resourcefulness and creativity emerged as Aria and I navigated the challenges of limited wardrobes. Each shared garment became a canvas for fashioning new combinations, reflecting our resilience in making the most out of what we had.

At the age of 14, my uncle granted me permission to work, providing me with a social security number that, although not rightfully mine, opened the door for employment opportunities. Securing a job happened almost instantly, and I found myself immersed in the world of work. The sense of independence and freedom that came with employment was exhilarating. Throughout the summer of 1997, I dedicated myself to work, relishing in the liberation it provided. Working those long summer hours wasn't just about earning money; it was about crafting a version of myself for the upcoming high school experience. Each shift contributed to the vision of stepping into September with a newfound confidence and a wardrobe that screamed, "I'm ready for anything!" The anticipation of transforming my appearance for the high school environment fueled my dedication to those long hours, shaping my financial independence and self-image.

During that year, I encountered Antonio—a man of undeniable charm and charisma. His infectious energy and quick wit drew me in, despite my lack of physical attraction. There was something magnetic about his personality that captivated me. It was during my ninth-grade year when Antonio first expressed interest in me. Regrettably, I declined his invitation, as I found myself inexplicably drawn to much older men at the time.

At the age of 14, I naively sought love and connection in the arms of men as old as 27, all the while oblivious to the potential dangers and consequences. As I reflect on my past, I am struck with both fear and gratitude.

Fear arises from the realization of the risks I exposed myself to during that vulnerable time, while gratitude fills me for the protection I was fortunate enough to receive. Desiring love and understanding, I ventured down a dangerous path where I allowed men to exploit my vulnerability and use my body for their own gratification. I am truly grateful for this stroke of fortune and the sense of protection I felt during those vulnerable years.

I'm grateful knowing that despite my innocence and the allure of attention from men, things didn't turn out worse for me because they could have. The allure of men and their promises clouded my judgment, leading to perilous situations. It's without a doubt that my youth's innocence and vulnerability were exploited, and consequently, the sexual assault caused emotional and psychological trauma. My youth's innocence and vulnerability were exploited, yet I am grateful to have evaded the harrowing fate that many others have not.

Reflecting on those times, I am filled with emotions—regret for the choices I made, relief for the protection I received, and a deep sense of gratitude for the resilience that carried me through. These memories serve as a poignant reminder of the fragility of youth and the importance of guidance and protection.

Antonio, my first love, reentered my life during high school, reigniting a connection that had started with his earlier proposal. The second time around, I decided to take the opportunity, and our journey together began. Coming from a large family, Antonio's charisma was undeniable, making our initial dates remarkably enjoyable.

As we ventured into our first date, his infectious personality overshadowed any reservations I might have had. There was an indescribable allure to Antonio, prompting me to overlook certain physical preferences and subtle warning signs. While he might not have fit the stereotypical image of what I considered my "type," a more profound connection began to blossom after a few dates. It wasn't just infatuation; I genuinely started to fall for Antonio. He had a unique way of making me feel special, and I found inspiration in witnessing the strong bond he shared with his family—at least, that's what I thought at the time.

At the age of 15, I lost my virginity to Antonio. At the time, he was 17, and we met at our usual spot in front of the school. It was a regular day, but something about it felt different. Antonio proposed an unconventional idea.

"Want to skip school?" he asked with a mischievous twinkle in his eye.

His question caught me off guard, and after a brief moment of consideration, I found myself agreeing. I knew I wasn't in the right headspace for school that day. The walk to his house, which was about 10 minutes away from our high school, was filled with excitement and nervousness. Along the way, Antonio revealed, "My older sister is home, so we'll need to sneak into the basement to avoid her catching us skipping school." The covert nature of our plan added excitement and secrecy, intensifying the emotions swirling within me.

Approaching his house, the anticipation of evading his sister and indulging in this rebellious act heightened the sense of adventure. Little did I know that this day would mark a pivotal moment in our relationship, forever etched in the memories of that turbulent chapter of my youth. We stealthily made our way through the back door entrance, which led directly to the basement. The air resonated with the loud music, some familiar beats of an Enrique Iglesias song echoing through the house. As we stepped in, darkness shrouded the basement, with a feeble light emanating from a flickering lamp in the corner. Antonio gestured for me to follow, and I obediently trailed behind him toward the back of the basement.

In the dimly lit room, I could make out a small bed, the sheets rumpled and inviting. "Let's just hang out here for now," Antonio suggested, but it was clear that there was more on his mind than just casual conversation. As he drew nearer, the atmosphere crackled with electric energy, and my heart accelerated in anticipation.

Suddenly, his lips were on mine, his tongue exploring my mouth with a fervent urgency. His hands traced over my body, igniting a fire within me as they moved from my breasts to the intimate depths of my being. Every inch of my skin felt burning hot, sending shivers down my spine as his fingers slid down from my chest, feeling my stomach all the way down between my thighs.

As he began to touch me, a rush of hormones overcame my senses, and I felt a heady mixture of desire and nervousness coursing through me. Soon his fingers trailed over my vagina as he looked at me and asked, "Are you ready?" My response was a breathless "Yes," my voice barely above a whisper.

At the age of 15, I experienced a significant change in my relationship with Antonio when I decided to be intimate with him. It marked the beginning of a pattern in which we would frequently skip school to seek moments of intimacy. Our rendezvous would take place at our school before our first period, and we would then go to his house, sneaking into the familiar confines of the basement. Over time, our secret meetings became a routine filled with passion and longing. The act of lovemaking, initially uncomfortable and uncertain, gradually became more familiar and less painful.

However, it lacked the overwhelming pleasure often depicted in others' stories. What brought me comfort was the connection I shared with Antonio. It was the feeling of being desired, touched, seen, and understood in a way that went beyond the physical act itself.

In those stolen moments, I found solace from the chaos of the outside world, a refuge where I could lose myself in someone else's embrace. It was a complex paradox - the fleeting delight of physical intimacy intertwined with a lingering yearning for something more profound. Nevertheless, in those stolen moments, I clung to the transient sense of belonging and being cherished as if it were a lifeline amidst an ocean of uncertainty.

My aunt eventually granted official permission for me to go out with Antonio, marking the beginning of our sanctioned dates. Every Friday, he'd show up in his vibrant red SUV, a uniquely customized vehicle adorned with stylish rims and captivating lights. The reggaeton beats emanating from his car became a distinctive signal of his arrival. As I heard Playero playing loudly, I rushed downstairs. I used to eagerly wait for the sound of his SUV's engine. As the beats of reggaeton echoed from his car, my heart fluttered with excitement. Antonio's arrival signaled the start of an evening filled with enchantment.

The unique aura of his vehicle mirrored the charisma he exuded, creating a sense of anticipation every time I walked down the stairs to meet him. The butterflies in my stomach were a testament to the thrill he brought into my life, a sensation unlike any I had experienced before. Antonio was a breath of fresh air, infusing our time together with fun and laughter. Our Friday nights became a ritual of joy as we immersed ourselves in the vibrant Latin community events – a fusion of music, dancing, games, and companionship.

Whether we were attending community gatherings or opting for a cozy movie night at his place, our bond deepened with each shared experience. Antonio had a magnetic ability to make every moment memorable, and those nights became the canvas on which our connection flourished.

December arrived, and with it came the unsettling realization that my period was overdue. Panic set in as I grappled with the gravity of the situation. Unlike previous instances of irregularity, this time was different – I was sexually active, and the stakes were higher. Unsure of what to do, I confided in Aria about the missed period.

Coincidentally, that day, both Aria and I were scheduled to work at McDonald's right after school. Sensing the urgency, Aria proposed buying a pregnancy test before our shift began. Hastily, I purchased the test, and as soon as we arrived at McDonald's, we headed straight to the bathroom. The seconds felt like an eternity as I anxiously peed on the test stick, my mind a whirlwind of thoughts and fears. Soon, as the pink lines began to appear, my heart sank. One line formed decisively, followed by the appearance of another faint but unmistakable line. The weight of the revelation hit me – I was pregnant. At that moment, the bathroom enclosed me, harsh fluorescent lights illuminating the small space. The sounds of the busy restaurant beyond seemed distant, as if the world had momentarily focused solely on the life-altering news I had just received.

As my gaze fixated on the pregnancy test, my mind raced with a multitude of uncertainties and questions. How would I disclose this to my uncle? What implications would this have on my future? Could I handle this? The reality weighed heavily upon me, casting a shadow over my familiar plans and aspirations.

Clutching the test strip bearing the undeniable truth, I turned to Aria, my trusted confidante in this sudden storm. "I'm pregnant," I uttered, the weight of those words hanging heavily in the air. Aria's immediate reaction mirrored the gravity of the situation.

"Oh shit," she exclaimed. The looming specter of parental disapproval haunted us. "Mami is going to kill you. Forget Mami. Your uncle is going to murder you," Aria remarked with concern and apprehension.

Our hushed conversation was interrupted by the arrival of our manager, a young, independent 18-year-old woman who had faced her own share of hardships. Recognizing the distress on my face, I mustered the courage to disclose my predicament.

As the words left my lips, tears flowed down my cheeks, a silent testament to the overwhelming emotions coursing through me. In that vulnerable moment, my manager extended a comforting hug, her words offering solace, "Take your time, sweetie." Those words became an unexpected refuge for me. In that moment of fear and uncertainty, the burden of the pressing need for decisions loomed over me. I decided to suppress those emotions and continued on with my duty. Enduring the lingering tension of my shift, I awaited the arrival of the evening when Antonio would pick me up, his car's familiar music signaling his approach. As I slid into the passenger seat, anxiety and nausea churned within me, anticipating the daunting revelation ahead. How would Antonio react? The question loomed in my mind like an ominous cloud.

Attuned to my subtle shifts in behavior, Antonio leaned over to kiss me, only to sense that something was amiss. The atmosphere in the car shifted as I presented the test strip, a silent harbinger of the life-altering news I was about to share.

"I'm pregnant," I confessed, uncertainty etched across my face.

Antonio, in response, exhibited a calm expression that momentarily overshadowed my inner turmoil.

"What are we going to do?" I questioned, seeking guidance in the face of an unforeseen future.

"Keep the baby, of course," Antonio asserted without hesitation. Yet, the weight of the decision lingered in the air.

"What do you want to do?" he inquired, inviting my perspective.

As I disclosed my truth, a complex mixture of emotions swirled within me. I was willing to take on the journey of parenthood, only on the condition that Antonio would commit to join me in facing the challenges that lay ahead.

In the ensuing days, the weight of uncertainty continued to bear down on me, wrestling with the decision to either embrace impending motherhood or proceed with a different path. Torn between choices, I found myself walking down the familiar street from my house to a nearby payphone. Summoning the courage to dial the number, I reached out to the Planned Parenthood clinic to secure an appointment for an abortion. The gravity of the decision hung heavily in the air as I steered the conversation, making a commitment to a choice that held both relief and a tinge of emotional turmoil. Having finalized the appointment, I retraced my steps home; the conflict within me was palpable.

As the evening approached, the time arrived for another shift at work; Antonio and I were slated to share the same workspace. I had helped him secure a job there about a month before I found out I was pregnant. I reached the workplace and entered the familiar stainless-steel kitchen, where Antonio was already immersed in preparing for the shift. I walked over to greet him, our eyes met, and he motioned for us to step outside for a quick conversation before our shifts started.

"Let's talk outside real quick," he said. We had barely 15 minutes to spare before our shift began.

"Yeah, sure," I agreed, and we headed out together.

Antonio looked at me with a serious expression and began to speak. He told me that he had been thinking a lot about our situation, and after careful consideration, he believed we should keep the baby. At that moment, Antonio's words hung heavy in the air, and his voice filled with conviction. He began expressing his thoughts, explaining how he had been contemplating our situation and believed we should keep the baby. It was clear that he held a strong opinion against abortions, as he shared his belief with me. As his words settled in, a rush of emotions overwhelmed me. Confusion, hesitation, and a flicker of hope stirred within me. Antonio's proposition seemed to offer a glimmer of a happy ending, a chance for the family I had longed for. Naivety washed over me, clouding my judgment as I eagerly responded, "Okay. Let's have a baby."

I was fully aware of the unrealistic expectations I had laid upon this decision as if it were the key to my happily ever after. Self-doubt crept in, questioning my own judgment. What was I thinking? Was I truly ready for the weighty responsibilities that motherhood would bring?

The complexities of trauma, survival instincts, love, and the power of manipulation intertwined, leading me to make the choice I did. It was a decision influenced not only by my own emotions but also by Antonio's influence and the foundation of his belief that guided my actions.

Antonio wasted no time in informing his parents about my pregnancy that very night. According to him, they expressed some disappointment and concern, yet offered their support. Meanwhile, I found myself unable to face my own aunt and uncle, needing more time to process, strategize, and formulate a plan for the uncertain future that awaited us.

Emotions swirled within me — apprehension, fear, and a glimmer of determination. I knew that I couldn't rush into any decisions hastily. A week passed by, and finally, I worked up the courage to share the news with my aunt. Spotting her sitting alone at the dining table, I waited for her to finish her dinner before approaching her. "Tia, there's something I need to tell you, and I'm afraid it will upset you." I took a deep breath and said as tears streamed down my face.

"What's wrong, Marihita?" she asked in Spanish with genuine curiosity in her voice. Marihita was the affectionate nickname used by everyone at home.

"I'm pregnant," I continued.

"What? Are you sure? How? When?" she exclaimed with evident shock in her voice.

Confirming that I was approximately six weeks pregnant, she immediately dialed my uncle's number. While I strained to hear their conversation, I noticed she simply mentioned that I needed to talk to him about something important later that night.

My uncle worked the evening shift as a chemical engineer at IBM, which usually ended around 11 p.m. My aunt came back into the room to inform me not to go to bed, emphasizing the necessity of discussing my circumstances with my uncle. Nervousness and fear gripped me as my stomach churned with unease.

The anticipation of speaking to my uncle grew with each passing moment. It felt as though my stomach had been punched, leaving me with a whirlwind of emotions.

Uncertainty loomed, and thoughts of his potential reactions consumed my mind. Would he be disappointed, angry, or understanding? These questions weighed heavily on me, intensifying the uneasiness in my stomach. The ticking seconds on the clock further heightened the tension in the room. The silence around me felt suffocating, magnifying my anxiety. The conversation with my aunt replayed in my mind, the shock in her voice and her immediate need to inform my uncle. It left me wondering how he would respond. Would he share the same emotions or perhaps surprise me with empathy? Only time would provide the answers.

The moment's significance became palpable as the clock drew closer to 11 p.m. Each creak and distant sound seemed to jolt my nerves. Restlessness took hold, and I found myself pacing back and forth, consumed by the approaching conversation.

Finally, the sound of the front door opening signaled my uncle's arrival. This was the moment I had been dreading and awaiting simultaneously. I heard my uncle's footsteps approaching the door as I lay in bed beside Aria in our shared room. Tension filled the air. Aria asked me if I was ready, and I nodded uncertainly. Gathering my nerves, I walked toward the kitchen, where my uncle was waiting for his food to warm in the microwave.

He sat down at the table with his plate in hand, unaware of the turmoil inside me. Curiosity etched his face as he noticed me approaching.

"What is it that you need to talk to me about?" he inquired as he took a bite.

"Tio, I'm pregnant." Nerves tightened my stomach as I found the strength to speak the heavy words burdening my heart. He blinked, his eyes widening with surprise. Swallowing his food, he greeted my confession with confused emotions. Soon, anger flared within him, expressed through a raised voice and intense words. The weight of disappointment hung heavily in the air. My heart sank as his words landed, their impact weighing on my conscience. Tears welled up, tinged with regret and remorse.

I tried to comprehend the depth of his anger, knowing it stemmed from concern and shattered expectations. Yet, understanding did little to ease the ache in my chest. The room fell silent, the space between us growing wider. I stood motionless, overcome by his disappointment.

Guilt, shame, and regret engulfed my emotions, each one a painful reminder of the choices I had made. The heaviness of the situation pressed down on me as though each word had become a physical blow. Tears streamed down my cheeks as I absorbed the weight of his disappointment.

In that moment, I longed for understanding, a glimmer of compassion that could bridge the gap between us. But the silence echoed in the room, signaling the difficulty of finding a resolution in such a heated exchange. I yearned for the opportunity to explain, to make him grasp the depth of my fear and uncertainty, but my words faltered.

"What were you thinking?" he asked, his voice filled with frustration and concern.

Those words were the only fragments I could discern amidst the heated exchange. From that point onward, I felt myself disengage, my mind tuning out the escalating chaos. Internally, frustration brewed, and I couldn't help but think, "What am I supposed to do now?" The only words seared into my memory were those spoken by my aunt. They collided with my emotions, intensifying my drive to pursue my education. My uncle presented me with two choices: to seek shelter with Antonio or to return to Honduras, where my father resided.

The prospect of going back to Honduras was out of the question; I firmly rejected the idea. At that time, my uncle had been in the process of adopting me to establish my legal status in the United States. However, he made it abundantly clear that he would no longer support this process. He uttered those words that felt like barbs penetrating my very being: "You are now on your own." Unsettling as it was, I had grown accustomed to feeling discarded, unwanted, and disappointing to those dear to me.

Despite the pain evoked by my uncle's words, I resolved to rise above the circumstances. I would utilize my emotions and reactions as motivators rather than allowing them to hinder me. This pivotal moment offered me an opportunity to reshape my life's narrative. With that resolve in mind, I wiped away my tears and took a deep breath as I silently promised myself that I would not let their perceptions dictate my future. Instead, I would utilize their doubts as fuel to prove myself and create a life that I could be proud of.

The following day, I mustered the courage to disclose to Antonio the conversation I had had with my uncle. It had become apparent that my uncle desired to confer with Antonio's parents concerning our predicament. With that in mind, Antonio and I made arrangements for his parents to come over to engage in a crucial discussion with my uncle. The day of the meeting arrived, and both hope and anxiety infiltrated the air. We had meticulously planned for this moment, hoping it would bring us clarity and resolution. Seated in my living room, we were greeted not only by Antonio's parents but also by his entire family - his four brothers and two sisters. Their presence filled the room, creating an atmosphere charged with expectation and concern.

As we settled into an uneasy silence, we waited for my uncle to join us, and time seemed to elongate endlessly. The weight of expectation bore down on us, and the absence of communication bred discomfort. An uneasy tension permeated the room, manifesting itself in furtive glances exchanged between those who were present.

Finally, after what felt like an eternity, my uncle made his entrance. He exuded a commanding authority as he entered the room, his aura radiating a sense of purpose and grit. However, his voice carried a subtle undercurrent of disappointment when he began to speak. The solemn tone penetrated the silence, leaving a lingering sense of regret hanging in the air.

My uncle, a man of great intellect, held education in the highest regard. It was a value he prioritized above all else, or at least that was the case during that particular time. His request, which he made during the discussion with Antonio's parents, was for me to stay in school and receive sponsorship from them.

I interpreted this as his way of demonstrating care and love, even if he never explicitly uttered the words "I love you." Deep down, I understood that he expressed his affection in his own unique way, grappling with his limited knowledge of how to show emotions and affection. My uncle's mindset had been shaped by societal conditioning and prevailing norms. He grew up believing in the notion that men should not openly display their feelings, that they must always project an image of toughness and avoid expressing vulnerability. He had unknowingly become a product of the patriarchal system, a system that disproportionately harms women but has also been shown to impact men. For men, it resulted in difficulty in fully articulating their emotions, leading to a disconnection from their own feelings. Seeking help or support was seen as a sign of weakness under this structure.

During that time, I failed to fully grasp the influences that shaped my uncle's thinking. It was only with hindsight that I began to understand the subtle impact of societal norms and expectations on his ability to express love and affection. The constrictions of gender roles had confined him, leaving him unsure of how to navigate the situations characterized by emotions and vulnerability.

Although our journey was marked with challenges, it is essential to recognize the underlying complexities that influenced my uncle's actions. While he may not have been able to communicate love overtly, his efforts to ensure my education and well-being were driven by a deeper sentiment. In his own way, he demonstrated love, albeit through a lens clouded by societal expectations and traditional gender roles.

When my uncle insisted that I leave behind the familiar confines of our home, it deeply wounded me. The thought crossed my mind that he was intentionally trying to punish me by stripping away all that was familiar and beloved. However, Antonio's parents stepped in to assure my uncle that they would assume complete responsibility for me, ensuring that my education would not be disrupted.

That very night, I departed with Antonio and his family, starting a new journey. The emotions I experienced during this transition were complex and profound. Leaving behind the life I had become accustomed to brought a deep sense of loss and sadness. Yet, there was also a glimmer of hope woven within the uncertainty of the future.

Chapter 7: Feeling like a Maid

Change had become a constant companion in my life, tossing me from one home to another since I was seven. But this time, the shifting tides felt different, unsettling. Sharing a bed with Antonio at fifteen felt strange, almost like stepping into a role society deemed too mature for my young years.

The first couple of months with Antonio seemed to go relatively well, or at least, as long as I submitted to his desires. A wave of sadness washed over me as he laid down the rule that I could no longer visit my own family. The words he spoke left a lasting mark on my heart, making me feel rejected and alone. It was a difficult truth to accept. Even though my family could visit me, I was not allowed to contact them, trapped under Antonio's power. The mere thought of their absence left an ache in the depths of my being.

My aunt and cousin came to visit me a few times during my pregnancy, providing brief moments of the love and connection I longed for.

Every day brought a whirlwind of emotions that threatened to consume me entirely. Sadness, resentment, and confusion mingled within, etching themselves onto my expression. I grappled with the internal battle between obeying Antonio's wishes and reaching out to the family I yearned to see. Gazing out of the windows, I felt an overwhelming sense of isolation as the world moved freely outside. The comfort of my family's presence and our daily routines now felt like a distant memory. Adult responsibilities weighed heavily on my fragile shoulders, contrasting with the carefree innocence my peers enjoyed in their youth. It was an existence I never anticipated nor desired.

My pregnancy wasn't the smoothest, but Antonio made an effort to offer support in his own way. The little bean in my belly wasn't making things easy. Throughout my pregnancy, I encountered a bunch of issues that made things really tough. From the get-go, I battled severe morning sickness for a whopping five months. Those days were a blur of nausea and exhaustion. Every bite felt like a betrayal, and my stomach twisted in revolt, even at the thought of food. Feeling sick all the time was a real struggle.

At that time, my doctor got worried because I wasn't gaining weight like I was supposed to. Instead, I even lost weight. This wasn't good for my baby, so my doctor referred me to a nutritionist.

Visiting the nutritionist brought both hope and fear. Could this really help me? Upon hearing my case, the nutritionist proposed a simple solution: indulge in fatty foods and satisfy my cravings.

Though almost too good to believe, I decided to give it a try. Pizza became my daily lunch, a remedy to the relentless morning sickness. Eating pizza every day did help with the sickness, but I didn't expect to gain weight so quickly. But that wasn't the only problem—I also had to deal with pre-eclampsia. My blood pressure was high, and I was swelling up. This worried both me and my doctor. It seemed like my body couldn't handle all these big changes. And there was more—I had to navigate cultural expectations, too. Antonio and his family believed in traditional values where women have to do a lot. Even though I was unwell, I had to wake up early, make breakfast, go to school, and then work. It felt like a never-ending cycle. Some days, even if I didn't work, I still had to come home and help with dinner.

I just wanted a break, a moment to take care of myself and my baby. But it wasn't that simple. I felt torn between what I needed and what society expected from me. My doctor told me to rest, but it seemed impossible with all the things I had to do. I was stuck between my health and what others wanted from me.

In my heart, I just wanted a break to take care of myself. But the reality was different. So, I kept going, doing what I thought was my duty and fearing disappointing others. In this battle between what my body needed and what society expected, finding a balance was hard. But I kept going, even if it meant not taking care of myself like I should have.

Antonio's older sister, Jessica, had already completed high school and wasn't engaged in work or further studies. As a result, she took on most of the household chores and cooking responsibilities. However, serving Antonio and his parents their meals fell under my responsibility, as I was told it was a cultural expectation.

At times, I longed to say no, but it felt impossible. On weekends, I had to rise early to prepare breakfast for everyone. Failing to do so would lead to a reprimand from Antonio's mother, creating a sense of pressure and obligation. I still remember a particular Saturday morning when Antonio's grandmother visited from Miami, Florida. Exhausted from managing school, work, and my pregnancy, I chose to sleep in.

Little did I anticipate that this decision would lead to an uncomfortable confrontation. I woke to the sound of Antonio's mother shouting downstairs, uttering hurtful words such as "She is so lazy" and "She should be up making my breakfast." She was complaining to Antonio's grandmother, who came for a brief visit, about me being lazy.

I wanted to make an impression on grandma, but Antonio's mother completely ruined it. She was throwing derogatory remarks at me in front of her mother-in-law, but grandma remained silent. This silence from Antonio's grandmother spoke volumes, leaving me feeling apprehensive about going down the stairs. I turned to Antonio, desperately seeking support, and asked him to accompany me, but he brushed me off, continuing to sleep. Anyway, I summoned the courage and bravely went down alone.

Upon arriving in the kitchen, I greeted Antonio's grandmother, who met me with a warm smile. My attention then shifted to Antonio's mother, who appeared visibly upset. Sensing the tension in the air, I said a hesitant "Good morning" and offered my assistance.

Accepting my offer, she replied with a curt "Yes," followed by a cutting remark emphasizing that I should have been the one preparing breakfast. Without responding back to her, I silently lowered my head and began helping her with the eggs, trying to hide any hurt or disappointment I felt. It saddened me to witness Antonio's mother speaking so poorly of me, someone who had worked hard to establish a harmonious relationship with their family. Yet, I remained steadfast, eager to dispel any lingering tension. As we worked side by side, Antonio's mother prepared

Baleadas, a traditional Honduran dish. Despite the tense atmosphere, I focused on my tasks, hoping my actions could ease some of the tension. By demonstrating respect and willingness to contribute, I hoped to mend the fracture that had strained the harmony within the household.

As my pregnancy progressed, the control exerted by Antonio and his family became increasingly overwhelming. Antonio's mother, with her firm beliefs about childbirth, insisted vehemently on natural birth, emphasizing that a "real woman" undergoes the entire process without any anesthesia. Her stories of delivering seven babies without medical interventions added to the pressure, creating a constant expectation for me to conform. In my desperate pursuit of acceptance from Antonio and his family, I lost touch with my authentic self, silencing my own voice.

Around the fifth month of my pregnancy, an exhaustion set in that made attending morning classes nearly impossible. The demands of my new life, coupled with responsibilities, left me physically and emotionally drained. Despite this overwhelming fatigue, I had to keep working to cover rent and basic needs. I had to pay $50 per week for the food and a roof over my head. These financial obligations were inescapable, forcing me to persevere. I found solace in the fact that Antonio's family provided me with food, a small comfort amid the challenges. Yet, despite gratitude for their provision, a sense of losing myself persisted. The constant pressure to conform gradually eroded my individuality, leaving me stifled and unheard. Balancing my desires with their expectations became really hard, leaving me torn and unsure of how to steer this new chapter. Deep within, I yearned for the freedom to be myself and to make choices aligned with my values and desires. Each day became a silent battle as I grappled with finding the strength to reclaim my voice while delicately managing the threads of a relationship and cultural expectations.

On August 12, it was time. I went into labor three weeks prematurely. I could feel the weight of impending contractions descending upon me, signaling that labor had begun. Promptly, we made our way to the hospital, where the doctor and nurses revealed their concerns about my high blood pressure. To mitigate any risks, they advised that I remain still in bed, limiting my movements. It was during this time that they presented me with the option of an epidural, a tempting prospect that promised relief from the impending pain.

Yet, deep within, I wrestled with conflicting emotions. Antonio's mother had instilled in me that a "real woman" delivers a baby naturally, unassisted by any medical interventions. Antonio, too, shared this perspective, reluctant to consider any form of pain relief for me. I allowed the opinions of those unaware of my pain to influence my decision, as I was young and easily swayed by others. However, looking back, I took responsibility for the choices I made, recognizing that I couldn't place blame elsewhere.

When the nurse approached me, offering the relief of analgesia through an IV, a glimmer of hope surfaced. She saw firsthand the discomfort plaguing me, understanding the possibility that I might not possess the strength required for the birthing process. In that moment, she became my unwavering advocate, my voice amidst the uncertainty. Firmly, she urged me to accept the analgesia, recognizing the necessity of my well-being. Even at that moment, I stared into Antonio's eyes and pleaded with him to allow me to take the analgesic. And thankfully, my plea for understanding was met with empathy. He, too, witnessed the profound pain etched upon my face and reluctantly agreed to the idea.

The emotions coursing through me during this pivotal moment defy concise description. Relief washed over me as the analgesia numbed the edges of my pain, easing the burden I carried. Yet, the flicker of guilt remained, tethered to societal expectations and the vulnerability that accompanied my choices.

After the IV Demerol kicked in, I fell into a deep sleep that gave my tired body a short break. When I woke up, the contractions hit me hard, making me toss and turn in pain. With every moment, the pain got worse, pushing me to a point of desperation. I realized I was getting close to full dilation, and all I wanted was relief from the agony.

I didn't care about Antonio or his family's opinions at that moment. I just wanted an epidural to ease the torment. Pleading with the nurse for any form of pain relief, I begged for a break from the relentless contractions. Sadly, her response shattered my hopes – it was too late. Despair filled me as I faced the reality that I had to endure the upcoming labor pains.

The doctor walked in, signaling it was time to start pushing. With each effort, my strength faded, leaving me drained and disheartened. The world's weight seemed to rest on my tired shoulders, and I doubted if I could endure any longer. The doctor's stern words cut through my exhaustion, emphasizing the importance of my efforts. "If you don't push," she warned, "no baby." Listening to those words, I summoned every bit of energy left in me. I found the strength for one last push. The feeling as my baby moved through my birth canal was both overwhelming and profoundly relieving. As he came into the world and was placed on my chest, a wave of relief washed over me. Seeing his beautiful eyes, a deep sense of awe and love surrounded me.

Yet, the exhaustion from the challenging process finally took over. Overwhelmed and drained, I gave in to unconsciousness, and my body surrendered to the relentless demands placed upon it.

Five days after giving birth, I returned home, eager to settle into a routine with our newborn. However, things weren't as I had hoped. Antonio wasn't very supportive during the nights. He expressed his need for sleep, fearing that it would affect his school grades. Although I understood his concerns, a quiet voice inside me questioned the toll it was taking on my own sanity. I felt a pang of loneliness in those dark, quiet hours. But in my submissive nature, I dare not question him just yet.

A week later, I started a new job at a telemarketing office despite my recent birth. The demands of work only added to the strains placed upon us. Antonio's behavior toward me began to change. He grew less affectionate and less present, his demeanor shifting toward control and irritability. The exhaustion shared between us as we passed sleepless nights cast a heavy shadow over our once-solid relationship.

Returning to live with Antonio, I yearned for the familiarity we once shared. But things were different now. He displayed more aggression and less patience toward me, mirroring my own growing frustration. I longed for his assistance during nighttime feeding sessions, desperately needing his presence and support. Yet, he continued to refuse, pushing the boundaries of our relationship.

One night, I gathered the courage to ask him to help with the baby at night. A simple request turned into a huge argument. In a moment of heated argument, our emotions spiraled out of control. Antonio's anger reached an alarming level, and in a fit of rage, he pushed me, causing me to collide with the door of our room. Shock washed over me, quickly followed by a torrent of tears. His behavior remained cold and unaffected as if our confrontation had never happened.

The warmth that once existed between us was fading, replaced by tension and aggression. I felt a growing distance, a sense that the person I thought I knew was slipping away. The tears on my cheeks mirrored the cracks forming in our relationship.

Antonio's sudden change in behavior started to take a toll on me. While he began spending more time with his friends on weekends, I was confined to the walls of our home.

The freedom to visit my own family was stripped away, replaced with the expectation that I could only socialize with his sisters. It felt suffocating as if I had lost all control over my own life. As the arguments escalated, I found myself bravely speaking up for myself, hoping to find some relief from this oppressive situation. To my dismay, my concerns were met with dismissal and disregard not only from Antonio but also from his family. My emotions were rendered insignificant, overshadowed by their complete invalidation.

The abuse crept into our relationship stealthily, beginning with verbal assaults. Antonio's words became daggers, thrown with precision and malice. Each time we argued, he hurled names at me like a venomous serpent. He cruelly branded me a fucking bitch, a whore, a nobody. His insults cut deep, leaving invisible scars that chipped away at my self-worth. He took pleasure in vehemently asserting that nobody wanted me, declaring that I was utterly worthless.

Initially, I absorbed his verbal abuse, paralyzed by the fear of being alone in a world that seemed increasingly hostile. But as time wore on, my strength swelled within me. I couldn't bear the name-calling any longer, so I made a conscious decision to stand up for myself. It was in that moment when I finally mustered the courage to call him a fucking asshole, to which his shock was palpable.

In response, Antonio tried to dominate me with his presence, stepping closer to intimidate me. But I refused to be cowed by his menacing tactics. Instead, I walked away, leaving him dumbfounded, lingering in the empty space I once occupied. Empowered by this act of defiance, I dared to believe that there was still a flicker of strength left within me.

The intensity of our arguments only heightened as time went on. I longed to go out with my cousin Aria, but Antonio vehemently refused to grant me that freedom. It was as if he felt that he owned me, that I was his possession, and he would not allow anyone else to share in my presence. Bit by bit, Antonio's controlling tendencies had severed the connections with my high school friends, leaving me isolated and alone. Jealousy consumed us both, but I was silenced, devoid of a voice that held any weight. My desires and opinions were consistently dismissed and discarded, further eroding my sense of self.

I felt trapped and suffocated by an invisible force that tightened its grip around me. A mixture of frustration, anger, and sadness swirled within my chest, threatening to engulf me. I felt an overwhelming desperation to go out, and tears flowed down my face as I begged Antonio to allow me this small freedom. But instead of showing compassion or understanding, my tears seemed to fuel his anger. He started calling me names, hurling hurtful words at me like venomous arrows aimed at my heart.

"You fucking bitch," he spat, his words laced with contempt. "You want to go whore around, don't you? That's what you're after?"

Enraged by his cruel words, I couldn't contain the anger brewing within me any longer. The phrase slipped from my mouth, unfiltered and raw, "You fucking asshole."

In that instant, his fury turned physical. A violent punch struck my face, causing pain to flare through my body, shock coursing through my veins. I found myself in his grasp, his hands entangled in my hair, as he callously threw me to the floor. The world seemed to freeze, and I lay there, stunned and disoriented. I couldn't believe what I had just experienced: the person I loved, the person who was supposed to care for me, had become a monster capable of such cruelty. Left alone on the floor, Antonio turned his back on me, and without a second thought, he exited the house, his car disappearing into the distance. I mustered the strength to drag myself upstairs to his sister's room, seeking consolation and understanding. The tears still streaming down my face, I poured out every detail of the abuse I had endured. To my surprise, both sisters expressed disgust at Antonio's behavior.

"It's not right what he did," Jessica said, her voice filled with empathy. "But you know how he is. He has a short temper. When he gets like that, just try to avoid him. Don't call him any names. Just walk away."

It was a horrifying realization to hear such advice, yet it seemed to align with the dynamics they had grown up with. As I learned, Antonio's father had been a man who both physically abused and cheated on his mother. The women in their household were forced into silence, their voices stifled, and their submission demanded.

The weight of this revelation settled heavily on my shoulders, mingling with the bruises that adorned my body. It was a reminder that the toxic patterns of behavior had been deeply ingrained within his family, creating a cycle that seemed almost impossible to break.

During those tormenting months, the arguments and vicious cycle of domestic violence became a harrowing routine. I endured it, absorbed it all, like a silent prisoner trapped within the confines of my own suffering. There were times when Antonio's idea of apology seemed to be rooted in sexual contact. He would whisper in my ear, his words laden with possessiveness, "Eres mía," claiming me as his own. This part is incredibly painful to recount, even now. But it is crucial to speak my truth, to acknowledge that I am not an isolated case. There are countless women out there who may be enduring similar experiences, often uncertain of how to label them.

We can find ourselves invalidating or minimizing our own feelings and truths, seeking protection within the confines of denial. The fear of confronting these uncomfortable emotions can be overwhelming. Yet, we must gather the courage to face our truths head-on, for there is no other way forward.

There were moments when I found myself actually welcoming Antonio's attempts to connect after the abuse. Simply because I craved that connection, mistaking it for love, believing that it would somehow fill the void within me. I also believed that love was sacrificing myself. But true, genuine love is not sacrifice. Genuine love is feeling safe and having the freedom to express yourself fully without fearing repercussions. Yet, there were also times when anger dominated my emotions when I couldn't bear to look at him or be near him. I would lie in bed, my back turned, silently yearning for him to stop touching me.

In the beginning, fear held me back from speaking up, asserting my boundaries, and telling him to stop. Alongside that fear, though, was a heavy dose of guilt. I believed that if I didn't please him or fulfill his desires, he would abandon me. His needs and wants always seemed to take precedence over mine, leaving me feeling powerless and voiceless.

So, I stayed silent, allowing him to roam my body, to take what he wanted without regard for my own desires. It seemed easier to endure his touch than to risk another argument or upset him in any way. I couldn't comprehend what was happening to me, the complex web of emotions that tangled within my being. The emptiness I experienced during those moments, the numbness that settled over me, became a defense mechanism. I didn't want to think about it — I simply submitted.

Suppressing everything seemed like the path of least resistance. I stooped low, shrouded in the aftermath of each form of abuse. The emotional and verbal abuse affected me most deeply, causing me to feel overwhelmingly alone, as if I didn't matter to anyone. I longed for someone to hold me, offer a comforting hug, and assure me that I was safe. Nobody uttered the words "I love you" or reminded me that the hurtful things said to me were far from the truth.

In those moments, I battled with a sense of worthlessness, convinced that the lashing out of Antonio's anger was somehow my fault. But the truth was far different. It was his pain, his unresolved trauma, that fueled his actions. If only I had understood that back then if only I had known my worth and the power of setting strong boundaries, I would never have betrayed myself. I would have honored my own needs and desires instead of pushing them aside for someone else's satisfaction.

It's important for me to acknowledge that, even though I may not have desired sex in those moments, what I truly craved was the feeling of being loved and connected, even if it meant compromising what my body didn't want.

The memories of this painful experience have long been shielded by my own mind as if protecting me from the full weight of the trauma. I can only recall fragments, like closing my eyes and succumbing to his desires for my body. I kept this to myself, afraid and ashamed. The confusion consumed me, leaving me unsure of how to process or even discuss what had happened. I yearned for someone to confide in, to release the pent-up emotions, but I couldn't trust anyone to truly believe me. And so, it stayed locked inside me, buried for years to come.

I couldn't help but blame myself. I allowed it to happen over and over again. It was my fault, or so I constantly reminded myself. It couldn't be coercion or assault, or so I desperately tried to convince myself. If I had allowed it, then how could I still care for him? Why did I possess an inexplicable desire to please him, regardless of my own feelings, wants, and needs? The gaslighting was real, distorting my perception and undermining my sense of self. This added to my confusion, making it even harder to label and understand what had befallen me. Even now, I wrestle with finding the right words to describe my experience.

Yet, there is one thing I know with certainty. There was an undeniable degree of coercion at play. I was manipulated psychologically and emotionally, whether intentionally or unknowingly. The power dynamics were skewed, and I found myself ensnared in its web. The subtle yet persistent pressure exerted upon me blurred the lines between consent and autonomy. It's an ongoing struggle, trying to navigate the complexities of these emotions and experiences.

I write about this now, allowing these thoughts and emotions to surface as part of my healing journey. It is not an easy task to express such deeply personal and raw moments, but I believe it is essential to shed light on the pain and confusion that survivors endure. The pain I feel in my chest is overwhelming. I am angry with myself for betraying my own boundaries and lacking self-love. It hurts deeply, and shame washes over me as I revisit this experience through my writing. But I know that in order to heal, I must allow myself to feel these emotions as I write. It's a moment of vulnerability that I choose to embrace.

Even though I may have forgiven him, the pain persists. It is a lingering ache that I tried to avoid for months, hesitant to confront it again. I feel ashamed that I allowed him to hold power over me for all these years. This wound runs deep.

I strive not to judge myself as I delve into these emotions and memories. I work on releasing the shame and guilt associated with writing about this part of my experience. There is a sense of guilt that arises from exposing this side of him. It stems from societal conditioning and the tendency to focus on the good aspects of a person. I always chose to see the good in him. But I now understand that his behavior was a manifestation of his own woundedness.

After I took a break from writing, I understood how important it is to let go of the pain, shame, and guilt that had been making me feel really bad. I found comfort in meditation, which helped me feel better and find moments of peace. I needed this time to deal with my feelings without being too hard on myself.

This part of my story, which I was unsure about sharing, is really heavy for me. I knew it would be tough to talk about such personal things, but something inside me told me to do it. I knew there were other people who could understand and needed to know they weren't alone. For three days, I spent a lot of time thinking about my feelings and facing them directly. I let out my pain through screaming, shouting, and crying, letting all those bad feelings come out of me. It was during this time that I started to see these feelings go away, losing their power.

Through meditation and connecting with my inner self, I realized some important things. I had been protecting myself for a long time by avoiding thinking about this tough time in my life. It was my way of keeping myself safe. When I thought about Antonio and his family, I saw that they didn't know about their own pain and actions. They were acting the way they did because of how they were brought up and the pain they carried. I understood that people who are hurt often end up hurting others without even knowing it. But I also saw how people who have healed can help others heal, too.

I'm writing about these experiences, using candid words to show how deep my feelings were. I hope that by sharing my story, others can get inspired to start their own journey.

A Message of Self-Reflection from My Higher Self:

Maria, I want you to know that it is indeed true that every person and situation in our lives can serve as a mirror, reflecting back to us the lessons we need to learn. In your case, you have to accept that sometimes these mirrors manifest through the demands of others, just as your in-laws and Antonio demanded so much from you.

Through these experiences, you have learned the importance of setting limits and boundaries. In other instances, mirrors appear through violence and mistreatment, allowing us to recognize the necessity of treating ourselves with compassion and kindness. It can also manifest through the disapproval or rejection of others, teaching us the importance of radical self-acceptance. Sometimes, it comes in the form of a lack of love or absence of affection, allowing us to understand the significance of self-love.

Often, we may believe that it is others who inflict pain upon us. However, beneath the surface, we discover that it is we who are hurting ourselves by abandoning our own needs and staying within a familiar yet hurtful space.

We convince ourselves it could be worse or that it's the best we can get. But what if we made different choices? What if we started being honest with ourselves and let go of the lies we have told ourselves to survive? Acknowledging and embracing awareness and honesty are vital steps toward healing.

Maria, you have been doing an incredible job of cultivating awareness within yourself. This is not an easy task, as it requires deep introspection and facing the pain head-on. You have reached a point where you can let go of blame and self-pity. Remember, you are not defined by what has happened to you. You are a creative, joyful, and playful being. Do not let years of conditioning convince you otherwise. Your strength knows no bounds, and you have the ability to overcome any obstacle in life. You are human, here to learn and grow. Therefore, have compassion for yourself, forgive your perceived past mistakes and choices, and continue to embrace and nurture your true self through self-connection.

Insights Gained Through Meditation:

In deep reflection during my meditation, a realization struck me with profound force. For years, I felt that Antonio held power over me, influenced by my own reluctance to let him go. Despite everything he had done to me, a part of me desired to maintain a friendship, to please him. I forgave him long ago, but the psychological impact lingered. I found myself trapped, feeling like his family's slave.

The wounds inflicted by this dynamic were excruciating. The pain cut deep, and it became clear that I struggled to release anyone who had hurt me from my life. This pattern, I now recognize, stems from the deep wounds of abandonment that I carry. Understanding who to let go of and who to be patient with is a process I'm currently undertaking.

It took me years to discover my worth, to discern what I deserve and what I don't. In the meantime, I remain resilient, knowing that healing and growth do not occur overnight. Time is a necessary ingredient, especially when the wounds run so deep. Some wounds demand extensive examination, unraveling their complex layers.

In our pursuit of healing, we often assign blame to a single person for the hardships we endure. Yet, my higher self, revealed through meditation, illuminated a crucial truth. I, too, have been heavily conditioned to believe that my wholeness and fulfillment rely upon the presence of someone else. As women, we have been indoctrinated with the idea that true connection can only come from a partner or another external source. We have not been taught how to forge deep connections with ourselves.

When do we reach a point in our lives when we stop sacrificing our own needs, wants, and desires for the sake of others? This question is rooted deeply within me. In my culture, men are often idolized, and we are conditioned to seek approval and permission from our fathers and husbands. The oppressive weight of macho culture bears down upon us, rendering women invisible in many ways.

However, at some juncture, we must shoulder the responsibility for our participation and actions in the reality we have created. Although I remained in this dysfunctional relationship for various reasons – financial security, immigration status, fear – I must also acknowledge my own dysfunctional role in the dynamics. I willingly handed over my power, continuously waiting for him to change, only to realize that change would never come, at least not with me.

Anyway, back to the story, I was falling behind in school due to an immense weight of stress bearing down on me. Balancing the demands of school, work, and my family life seemed like an insurmountable challenge. The stress levels were overwhelming, leaving my nervous system dysregulated. Sleep became a precious commodity, with my son keeping me awake for most nights. He had his days and nights confused, making it even more difficult for me to get the rest I needed.

During the day, Jessica took care of my son while I attended school. She mentioned that all he did was sleep, waking up only briefly for meals before dozing off again. However, it was during the nights that I bore the brunt of exhaustion. Finding the time and mental energy to study became nearly impossible. My responsibilities at home were relentless – cooking dinner, caring for the baby, and serving dinner for my in-laws and Antonio. Once dinner was over, I had only a few hours left to catch up on homework and study. Fatigue consumed me.

On the days I worked after school, I hardly had any time to spend with my son. I would eagerly try to put him to bed early, but he resisted, wanting to stay awake and play. I couldn't resist those precious moments with him; he was my light, my love, and my reason to keep going. He became my greatest motivation not to give up. I would stay up with him, feeding him, playing with him, and trying to lull him to sleep. He relished our time together, almost as if he understood that it was the only time he had with me, his mother. Our nights often stretched into the early hours, with him finally succumbing to sleep close to 5 a.m.

Every night, I would watch Antonio sleep peacefully while I remained awake, tending to our son's needs. His excuse was always that he had school in the morning. Well, so did I, but it seemed that my own responsibilities were inconsequential in his eyes.

The emotions attached to these experiences were deeply intense. The stress, exhaustion, and longing for quality time with my son created a rollercoaster of emotions within me. Despite the challenges, I carried on, fueled by the love and connection I shared with my son, even with fatigue and sacrifices.

I struggled to get out of bed some mornings, feeling utterly exhausted. As a result, I would occasionally miss my morning class and only make it to school for the second period. The situation at home was deteriorating rapidly, turning into a genuine nightmare. Conflict seemed to be mounting at every turn. Antonio and I found ourselves engaging in more frequent and intense fights. According to my in-laws' expectations, the role of a woman was to be submissive and docile, to remain in her designated place. Expressing my opinions or raising my voice was heavily frowned upon. Frustrated with these constraints, a rebellious streak began to emerge within me. My fight-or-flight response was on high alert, fueling my reactions. I resorted to shouting and calling Antonio names in response to his derogatory remarks. The anger radiated within me, and I let it explode as I screamed, "You fucking asshole!" This only served to further infuriate him.

Escalating the conflict, he resorted to physical violence once again, striking, beating, and knocking me to the ground. In those painful moments, there were times when I simply remained on the floor, absorbed in tears of despair. Yet, there were also instances when a surge of inner strength compelled me to rise and retaliate. I would throw punches at him, targeting his back in my attempt to hurt him as he had hurt me. He always insisted on having the last punch, but that didn't deter my determination. At that moment, I ceased to care about the consequences; all I wanted was to inflict the same pain upon him that he inflicted upon me.

Chapter 8: Living with an Abusive Partner

Another year had quietly slipped by, leaving behind an eerily familiar sense of stagnation. This was the year I had anticipated, the year of my long-awaited graduation. As a senior, my schedule was packed with classes that were meant to propel me toward a brighter future. Antonio, on the other hand, had already graduated the year before and had secured a full-time job, earning a decent income. Unfortunately, a significant portion of his earnings still went toward supporting his family, leaving us with a meager amount to set aside for our own dreams of a modest apartment.

Antonio's devotion to his family was undeniable, as they held a significant place in his heart. However, I couldn't help but wonder if I truly fit into that cherished image of his loved ones. Doubts often plagued my mind, casting uncertainty on whether he saw me as a part of his family. It was a puzzling contradiction. How could someone who demonstrated such anger and violence toward me also claim to love me deeply?

With time, I began to grasp a glimmer of understanding. I started to unravel the complexities hidden beneath his outward expressions of anger. It became clear to me that his anger was not truly directed at me but rather at himself and, perhaps, at his father. It seemed to be a manifestation of his inner turmoil, a storm that raged inside him. Although it was painful to bear the brunt of his anger, I slowly understood that it was not fundamentally directed at me. I became an unfortunate target of his pent-up frustration and unresolved conflict.

Even so, this realization did little to mitigate the pain and scars etched upon my heart. Love should never be tarnished with violence or laced with such agony. Yet, paradoxically, I held onto the belief that Antonio did harbor a love for me, albeit one entangled in a web of self-loathing and tumultuous emotions.

Love, as I soon discovered, exists in shades of complexity. It intertwines light and darkness, tenderness and pain. Antonio's love trod the fine line between these dichotomies, often on the precipice of something unknown. While it was a challenge to comprehend and accept, I acknowledge the depths of his emotions and the unusual bonds that tied us together – it was a trauma bond.

And so, I proceeded cautiously, bracing myself for the storms that periodically raged while clinging to the belief that somewhere deep within him, an authentic love existed, however obscured.

As the months passed, our arguments escalated, each teeming with an overwhelming influx of hurt and anger. It seemed as if we were both weighed down by the weight of our respective pain. Antonio, in particular, appeared to carry a deep-seated anger toward the world, easily provoked by even the slightest triggers. Every day felt like a minefield, as if I had to tiptoe on fragile eggshells around him and his family. The fear of setting off his anger overshadowed my ability to express myself freely and embrace my own existence.

My voice, more often than not, was silenced. My opinions held little weight, overshadowed by the question: "What does Antonio think?" It was as if my own thoughts and beliefs held no significance. My frustration grew as I yearned to assert myself and declare, "What does Maria want and believe?" But the desire to be accepted and liked by his family kept me quiet, my true, authentic self slipping further into the shadows. I found myself hiding behind a facade, concealing aspects of my being in the hopes of gaining approval.

Feelings of insignificance and unworthiness became familiar companions. It seemed as if I were constantly reminded of my status as an outsider, never truly a part of the family. The weight of being seen as the "other" bore down on me, leaving me feeling small and insignificant in the world that enveloped that house. In their eyes, I was less than, always relegated to the sidelines, perpetually yearning for acceptance and validation. It was a lonely path to tread, one filled with emotional turmoil and a constant battle with the sense of self. I longed for a space where my voice would be heard, my opinions valued, and where I could wholeheartedly embrace my worth.

There's a limit to the darkness one can endure. And I was slowly losing my patience. I have been silently taking all this darkness in for such a long time. But, in between that dark period, there comes a point where the burden becomes unbearable. It felt like I was standing at a crossroads, with two paths in front of me to choose from. One to keep on treading the hurtful path and the second to face this darkness head-on. I have no idea where I got my gut of steel and what triggered it, but I decided to fight back using my words.

I made the decision that I won't take the verbal abuse silently anymore. Speaking up for me became a way for me to regain power and control. I still can't figure out where that courage came from, but all I know is that it was so strong that I stopped caring for the consequences my words or actions could bring. It was like a rebellion against the darkness and my surroundings. I started expressing my thoughts without holding back.

The fear of physical pain slowly faded away, replaced by a burning desire to express my true self, to assert my existence in a world that often tried to ignore it. I knew my words wouldn't have much effect, but speaking my mind felt like a small victory. It wasn't about fighting the darkness around me. It was just a fight that I put up against the darkness, refusing to let it consume me fully.

One time, Antonio and I were caught up in a big argument. I can't remember exactly what we were arguing about, but I remember clearly what happened next. Things got really intense quickly. He started calling me names and saying hurtful things with so much anger. I didn't stay quiet either and said some hurtful things back.

We became increasingly emotional, and our voices grew louder as we descended the stairs. It felt like our anger was taking over the whole basement of Antonio's parents' house. I was holding my one-year-old son and following Antonio closely. I was so mad, sad, and shocked. I was gritty not to back down, but I didn't know our argument would turn violent.

I didn't realize it, but my words must have really upset him. I didn't see it coming when Antonio suddenly stopped and then swung his fist at my face. Everything felt like it stopped as his punch hit my cheek. I was shocked and couldn't believe what had just happened. I held onto our child, protecting him from getting hurt. It was so sudden that I wasn't able to think clearly for a moment. I felt a mix of disbelief, pain, and confusion. How could he hit me while I was holding our son? It hurt me a lot and I was struggling to understand what had just happened.

My cheek hurt so much, and I felt the bruise starting to form. The pain from the punch throbbed on my cheek, reminding me of the emotional pain we had been going through. My face showed the mark of his violence, but inside, I was feeling a storm of emotions.

I was consumed by anger. So much so that I dashed upstairs, plunked my son in his highchair, grabbed a knife from the kitchen, and went back downstairs. I stood by the door, the knife clenched in my hand, ready to confront him. He was about 10 feet away from me, just staring at me with those cold, emotionless eyes. I wanted to end him right then and there.

At that moment, a desire to harm him coursed through me, but I couldn't bring myself to follow through. It was like something inside me held me back. I retraced my steps to stow the knife away upstairs and then returned to the basement. I wasn't thinking clearly, but my purpose remained the same. As I reached the bottom of the stairs, he was waiting by the door.

As soon as he saw me, he exploded. He started punching my head, his fists flying in a blur of rage and fear. I stumbled back, trying to defend myself, but the blows kept coming. All I could do was shield myself and try to protect my head. Eventually, he stopped, giving me a small window of opportunity.

Summoning every ounce of strength, I delivered a powerful punch to his back, visibly eliciting pain. Yet, before I could react further, he seized me by the hair, forcefully hurling me to the ground. The onslaught persisted, with his rage mercilessly directed at my body and head. Fear, anger, and desperation overwhelmed me as I lay there, desperately attempting to shield myself from his brutal barrage, rendering the encounter a nightmarish ordeal that left me feeling utterly powerless.

I instinctively shielded my head on the floor. Fueled by adrenaline, the immediate pain of the assault eluded me. However, after a few minutes, the realization struck like a sudden wave—a sharp headache set in, accompanied by a noticeable hearing loss in one ear. Bruises adorned my face and arms, tangible evidence of the brutal attack. Overwhelmed and unsure of how to proceed, I sat on the floor, face down, tightly hugging my knees while rocking back and forth. Confusion and desperation washed over me as I grappled with the aftermath of the assault.

After a few minutes, lacking direction, I mustered the strength to rise and made my way to my neighbor Krista's house, who was my sole friend at the time. Feeling scared and alone, I struggled to make sense of the situation. The bruises made me feel small, hurt, and lost in a sea of emotions.

Arriving at Krista's home, I felt relief seeing someone who cared. She was furious at Antonio, urging me to go to the hospital and report him to the police. As time elapsed, the intensifying pain in my ear prompted me to follow Krista's advice and seek assistance at the hospital.

At the hospital, the diagnosis revealed a ruptured eardrum, underscoring the severity of the injuries I had sustained.

Confronted with this grim reality, I made the challenging choice to press charges against Antonio, aiming to hold him responsible for his actions. As a result, he was taken into custody and ultimately sentenced. Throughout the ordeal, I found it unsettling that Antonio never once mentioned the knife that I had pointed at him, opting to remain silent on the matter.

This incident left me without a place to call home. After my hospital visit, the police accompanied me to Antonio's house to pick up my son. I had nowhere to go. I was once again left homeless. Feeling desperate and without options, I reached out to my cousin and Aunt from Plattekill, NY, hoping they would allow my son and me to stay with them. I called them and explained my situation, and fortunately, my aunt agreed to help us. She kindly came to pick us up, as I had no means of getting there myself.

During this challenging time, money was a constant concern. I wasn't working at the time, and I had no savings. Thankfully, my aunt generously offered to pay for my antibiotic prescription for my ear infection, understanding the urgency of my health situation.

The next day, Antonio was released from jail after posting bail. This news brought forth a whirlwind of emotions. I felt a mix of relief and anxiety, unsure of what the future held for us. It was a temporary reprieve, as a hearing was scheduled for the following week to address his case.

In the midst of this chaotic situation, the threats of calling immigration were constantly looming over me. These threats came from him and his family, and though they were unsettling,

I knew they wouldn't hold much weight. Regardless, I had already made up my mind to drop the charges. Especially when he never brought up the knife incident. At that moment, I feared things could have turned sour for me. My feelings toward him were complex - a mix of hatred and love. Despite the hardships, we shared some good moments together. However, it was evident that both of us had limitations in our thinking and way of being.

Our actions stemmed from a place of deep wounds and unconsciousness. A conscious and aware individual would recognize that we are all mirrors of one another. Our thoughts and triggers are reflections of our inner worlds. When we inflict harm upon each other, we inadvertently hurt ourselves in the process. It's a cycle that perpetuates pain and suffering. This realization added another layer to the complicated emotions I carried during that time.

Well, I must say that escaping an abusive relationship isn't a straightforward journey. For many victims, like Antonio's mother, it might take multiple attempts or, sadly, never happen. Abusive relationships are like tangled webs, incredibly complex and challenging to solve. It demands immense courage to break free, to realize that you deserve more than the life you've been living.

Leaving becomes even more difficult when you've grown up surrounded by abuse when it feels like a familiar part of life. Understanding what a healthy relationship looks like becomes a daunting task. Factors like low self-esteem, intimidation, shame, fear, lack of resources, absence of support, immigration status, children, and, yes, even love contribute to why a victim might stay trapped in an abusive relationship.

It's not just a matter of walking away; it's about untangling a lifetime of emotions and expectations and breaking free from the chains of fear and insecurity. Each step toward leaving is a battle against the familiar, a step into the unknown. Yet, it's a journey worth taking, a journey toward reclaiming one's worth and finding a path to genuine love and safety.

In my case, my immigration status and low self-esteem posed significant obstacles to me becoming self-sufficient and independent. The fear of being alone often consumed me. I would constantly worry that nobody would ever want someone like me. Deep down, I felt completely worthless. I lacked the belief in myself, or at least not yet. Eventually, I decided to move back in with him.

The idea of being alone seemed like a daunting abyss, pushing me to doubt my own value. The internal struggle intensified, making it hard to resist the pull back into a relationship that, despite its toxicity, felt like a familiar, albeit painful, haven. The decision to move back with him became a compromise, a desperate attempt to escape the overwhelming fear of isolation.

It was like I was caught in a cycle perpetuating the narrative of unworthiness and dependence. Each step forward felt like a battle against the shadows of doubt, and in those moments, the temporary solace of a familiar but harmful embrace seemed like the easier choice.

I recently had a conversation with Jennifer, Antonio's sister-in-law, about our past together, and it brought up some painful memories that I had long forgotten. She herself had faced strong disapproval from Antonio's family and had a particularly challenging time living in that household. She described with haunting clarity the moments when I would scream, and she admitted feeling utterly helpless. She recalled shutting her bedroom door, desperate to block out the sounds, yet unable to shake the echoes of my pain. I hold no blame toward her, for she herself carried her own deep scars from those days.

Jennifer's words brought back a flood of forgotten instances, moments that my mind had mercifully shielded me from. One memory stood out vividly, as if time had frozen, etching it permanently into the fabric of my being. One memory resurfaced with startling clarity when Antonio, the person responsible for my suffering, left his handprint on my face. The pain and humiliation I felt on that day came flooding back.

During the conversation, another incident resurfaced, one that I had buried far beneath layers of shame and humiliation. I had managed to bury them away, perhaps as a form of self-protection. Jennifer's words acted as a catalyst, stirring forgotten recollections from the depths of my mind. Antonio's merciless blows had left me with a swollen, bruised eye, almost swollen shut. I remember being unable to open my eye properly, as it was almost swollen shut from the beating I had endured.

Jennifer mentioned being able to see the broken blood vessels in that eye - a clear indicator of the severity of the injury. It was a subconjunctival hemorrhage inflicted by punches to my eye. This medical term seemed too clinical to encapsulate the pain and fear that coursed through my veins. In the aftermath of that particular episode, an overwhelming sense of shame washed over me. The thought of facing the outside world, attending school, and exposing my battered self to the judgment of others seemed unbearable. I felt too ashamed to face my classmates, so I made the difficult decision to skip school for days on end.

I made the painful decision to withdraw, to remain hidden away. The days turned into weeks as I absented myself from the classroom until the accumulation of my absences reached a critical point, forcing the school to take action, leading to my eventual expulsion.

In the end, I had to deal with the results of my decisions. I had to retake the same classes in the summer to make up for the ones I missed. It was tough to catch up. The cycle of abuse not only left physical scars but also disrupted the rhythm of my education, a poignant testament to the far-reaching consequences of domestic violence.

Chapter 9: Fresh Start

Life seemed promising as Antonio, our son, and I settled into a cozy one-bedroom apartment in a neighboring town just across the Newburgh-Beacon Bridge. This move came after a recent confrontation with Antonio's mother, which resulted in me being kicked out of their house. Unfortunately, Antonio's family profoundly influenced our relationship, particularly his parents, who I saw as rather unkind individuals.

My feelings toward Antonio's parents were undoubtedly colored by the way they had mistreated both Jennifer and me over time. It seemed as though compassion was a foreign concept to them; they lacked the ability to empathize with the struggles and challenges faced by others. Their actions and words consistently revealed a callousness that left a bitter taste in my mouth.

The way they treated Jennifer and me was particularly disheartening. It felt like we were constantly scrutinized for every decision and action. They seemed to derive satisfaction from tearing us down, their criticisms cutting deep into our hearts. It was exhausting and emotionally draining to consistently come up against their harsh judgments.

Their lack of compassion extended beyond just their words. They showed little interest in understanding our perspectives or providing any support during difficult times. Instead, they seemed to revel in highlighting our flaws and shortcomings as if it gave them some perverse sense of superiority. Their behavior left me hurt, angry, and deeply resentful toward them.

Living under their influence felt suffocating. We were constantly walking on eggshells, afraid to make any misstep that would ignite their wrath. Their presence loomed over our lives, casting a shadow of negativity and distrust. It was a toxic environment that made it difficult to find joy and happiness in our own little space.

Life seemed promising once again as we found our own space away from Antonio's family. Despite the terrible behavior of Antonio's family, they were human, and being human means we all have the capacity for wrongdoings. They carried unresolved trauma deep within themselves. They were also deeply attached to their cultural conditioning and traditions, which shaped their behaviors and actions.

In all honesty, I used to blame them for everything. I couldn't help it. However, I now understand that our treatment of others often reflects our awareness and inner state. It became clear to me that they were all hurting, carrying a tremendous amount of pain, particularly Antonio's mother.

Her pain manifested in her actions and words, vibrating intensely. You could feel the weight of it in the atmosphere. Her eyes held a tinge of sadness and weariness, mirroring the weight she carried. Lines etched deep on her face revealed the struggles and heartaches she endured. Her brows were often furrowed, expressing constant concern and worry.

Even her movements seemed burdened, as if she carried an invisible load, each heavy step lifted with effort. Her gestures were filled with tension, as if she was trying to contain the immense pain within her.

And then there were her words. They were often laced with bitterness, a result of the suffering she had endured. They could be sharp and cutting, leaving wounds, or resigned, as if she had given up hope of finding true happiness.

Reaching this understanding wasn't easy for me. It required looking beyond the surface and recognizing the hidden pain they carried. I no longer hold blame in my heart; instead, I've gained a more profound empathy for them. I see now that their cultural conditioning and loyalty to tradition offered solace and identity in the face of life's challenges. I realized that they were simply hurt souls trying to navigate life the best way they knew how. While it doesn't excuse their actions, it allows me to view them with a greater understanding.

So, in the end, I choose to embrace empathy and compassion for Antonio's family. Recognizing their pain has transformed my perception, cultivating empathy and compassion toward them.

A few months passed, and things between Antonio and me appeared to be somewhat better during that time. We still had our fair share of small arguments, but thankfully, the physical abuse had come to an end. At this point, I was just 18 years old, and unfortunately, I hadn't yet graduated with my class. I was a few classes short, meaning I had to attend summer school at that time and night school in September to make up for it. It wasn't the ideal situation, but it was the path I had to take to obtain my high school diploma.

The emotions I experienced during this time were a blend of disappointment and determination. It was disappointing not to be able to graduate alongside my peers as I had initially hoped.

Seeing my classmates move on while I had to tackle additional schooling during the summer was disheartening. However, I also felt a strong surge to overcome this setback and complete the remaining classes. I knew that this setback wouldn't define my future. It was a temporary obstacle that I needed to overcome. I was determined to put in the effort, attend summer school diligently, and complete those remaining classes.

And to stay true to my resolve, my actions spoke volumes. I attended every class, completed assignments on time, and sought assistance whenever needed. There were moments of frustration when certain lessons proved challenging, but I persevered, knowing that each hurdle conquered brought me one step closer to graduation.

We lived around a 10-minute drive away from my high school, but at that time, I didn't know how to drive. As a result, I relied on Antonio to take me everywhere. Our routine involved Antonio dropping off our son at the babysitter and then driving me to school early in the morning so that he could make it to work on time. Unfortunately, he couldn't pick me up in the afternoon due to his full work schedule. This meant I had to walk for nearly an hour to my home, pushing my son in the stroller across the Newburgh-Beacon Bridge every day until summer school ended in August.

During this time, I was exhausted. All this physical and mental pressure was taking a toll on me. My body used to give in, but my heart and mind were resilient. I felt a burning desire to complete my summer school classes to finally obtain my high school diploma. It was a goal I held close to my heart, so despite the challenges, I was determined to push through.

I would wake up early each day and prepare myself for another long walk home. The heat of the summer sun beat down on me as I pushed the stroller across the bridge, the weight of my son adding physical strain. Sweat trickled down my forehead, and my body ached from the exertion, but I pressed on.

The strain and fatigue were evident, but so was my unwavering resolve to succeed. I couldn't afford to give up or let exhaustion consume me. My goal of obtaining that high school diploma fueled my actions, and every step forward was a testament to my determination. It was a challenging and tiring experience, but my resolve to complete my diploma motivated me to endure it all.

I was dead set on not becoming another teenage mom dropout, just like my aunt had predicted. So, I pushed myself hard. I wanted to show everyone, especially my family, that I wasn't some screw-up. I had this burning need to prove that I could be smart and successful, no matter what life had dealt me. Why did I care so much? Probably because deep down, I just craved to be seen by my family. I wanted someone to be proud of me.

Every day, when I dragged myself through that long walk with my son in tow, it wasn't just about crossing a stupid bridge. It was my way of saying, "Look, I'm doing this. I'm working hard, and I'm not giving up." The sweat on my forehead and the ache in my body were like badges of determination.

When I limped across that bridge, I wasn't just pushing a stroller. I was pushing against the expectations people had for me. I was proving that I wasn't just some stereotype. There was this frustration and grit on my face. It wasn't glamorous; it was real life, replete with struggles and messy hair. I didn't want to be the girl people whispered about, the one who messed up big time. I wanted to be the one who surprised everyone, who flipped the script. Maybe deep down, I was shouting, "See? I'm not just another statistic. I'm doing something with my life."

Emotions? Oh, they were all over the place. There was this mix of determination and fear of being seen as a failure. Every step I took felt like a statement – a declaration that I could beat the odds.

Yes, I was exhausted, but there was a spark of stubbornness. I wasn't about to let anyone write me off. I dragged myself out of bed every morning, preparing for this marathon walk. The pushing, the sweating, the sore muscles – it was all part of the journey. And all the while, there was a fire inside me that needed to break free from the stereotype that kept me going.

Why did I want it so bad? It was simple. I wanted my family to look at me and say, "Hey, she did it. She didn't let life knock her down. We're proud of her." That was the driving force, the fuel that kept me going through those long walks, through the sweat and exhaustion – just wanting someone, somewhere in my blood, to be damn proud of me.

Finishing high school felt like this golden ticket to finally getting some love, respect, and approval from my family. A diploma was my ticket to being seen as someone worth their attention. My uncle was all about education and success, and I caught that bug from him. I looked up to him for that. I liked how he valued education.

I used to think things would magically change if I just got that piece of paper. Every assignment and test felt like a step closer to being "good enough" for my family. It wasn't about being a genius but proving that I could stick it out and be something.

I admired my uncle for having this mindset of prioritizing education and qualifications. I wanted him to like me and be proud of me. There was this desire inside me, a wish to earn his approval. So, graduating high school became this goal, this way to measure up and, hopefully, make my family look at me with the love that I yearned for.

I now understand that our society emphasizes success and education, leading us to measure our value by career achievements and financial gains. It's not like I'm against any career progress or anything. It's just I want you all to realize that career and financial gains are just a part of your life, not the only thing your life should revolve around.

On a personal level, my success is tied to the depth of my connection with myself. The deeper I connect with my inner being – my higher self, the more I elevate my consciousness. We have all the answers within, and as we reach a higher state of consciousness, we realize that time is an illusion and the only true moment we have is the present moment. Therefore, success for me means fully immersing myself in the experience of the present moment, savoring every second of the now, and expressing the most authentic version of myself.

But back then, graduating was like my only mission. So, I became a pro at shoving all my feelings down and zoning in on that finish line. No time to feel anything – just laser focus on the goal. But little did I know, it was like setting up a time bomb, just ticking away until it decided to blow. This constant battle was inside me – the need to finish school versus all these feelings I buried deep. Suppressing stuff took its toll, and I felt like a ticking time bomb, just waiting for that explosion. In every situation, even in tough times, I'd smile and act like everything was cool, but this storm was brewing underneath. It was like holding back a tidal wave of emotions with a paper dam.

I had a robotic routine – wake up, go to school, study, repeat. No time for emotions, just the grind. Until, of course, it all caught up with me. I went on like an emotionless robot. Because back then, graduating felt like the lifeline. Little did I know, a storm was brewing inside me. It was like I put all my feelings in a pressure cooker, and when the lid finally blew, it was messy. But at the time, all I wanted was that diploma, so I gritted my teeth, suppressed my feelings, and pushed forward, not realizing the storm it was stirring up inside me.

I bottled those feelings, thinking I could shove them in a mental box and call it a day. But that box wasn't built to last. Time passed, those buried emotions were a ticking time bomb, and the countdown was on. And soon, I faced the consequences of my actions. These pent-up emotions exploded, demanding attention in ways I never expected and impacting both my body and mind severely.

The repercussions of those suppressed emotions manifested in various ways, both physically and emotionally. Emotionally, I felt overwhelmed and mentally drained. I experienced moments of frustration and doubt, wondering if I could truly push through the challenges that lay ahead.

Chapter 10: The End of a Toxic Relationship

Graduating felt like a significant win, a victory dance in early January of 2001 when that high school diploma finally landed in my hands. I was over the moon. But the joy train took a detour when Antonio dropped the bomb – we were moving back to his parent's place to save money. It hit me like a ton of bricks, and suddenly, my world crumbled.

I felt sick at the thought of heading back to that house, a place crammed with memories I'd rather forget. I was crushed - like, stomach-churning, heart-sinking kind of crushed. The memories of that house – oppressive moments – were a real horror show. Nightmares played in my head, and I desperately wanted to avoid that house of horrors. All I could feel was the weight of going back to a place I never wanted to see again, hoping against hope that things would somehow turn around.

I could practically taste the disappointment in the air. My dreams of freedom, of breaking away from that past, shattered. It was like going back in time to a place I desperately wanted to escape.

Still trapped with no better options, I clung to a small hope that maybe, just maybe, Antonio would change and help me get some stability. I was distressed, but the hope was still there, lingering like a stubborn ghost. I clung to it, thinking maybe, just maybe, Antonio would have a change of heart. Maybe he'd step up, help me get that permanent residency, and we'd finally move on to a better chapter. Packing up my stuff was like prepping for a journey into my own personal nightmare. Each step toward that house felt heavier, like stepping into a past I wanted to leave behind. The place seemed to mock me, the familiar facade holding all the fears and anxieties I tried to escape.

Inside that house, the air felt thick with memories, squeezing me with their weight. Walls closing in, the smell of old memories was like I time-traveled to the moments I desperately wished to forget.

Living there was like an emotional battlefield. Those days were a mess of emotions – a tug-of-war between reflection, frustration, and that tiny glimmer of hope kept me going. Each passing day was a reminder that change was overdue, that I had to find my own path away from the horrors of that house and move toward a future where freedom and happiness weren't just distant dreams.

A few months had passed since our return to Antonio's parent's house, and the fact that we still weren't married weighed heavily on my mind. I felt the need to begin pressuring Antonio once again, reminding him of his promise to help me attain legal status. I suggested that one way he could assist me was by helping me find a job. We began discussing the possibility of obtaining a social security number, which would enable me to start working.

The thought of having a job became increasingly important to me as a potential safeguard in case the recurring abuse I was experiencing escalated. I knew that having a source of income would provide me with the means to leave the situation if necessary. This realization made the pursuit of a social security number even more urgent. Antonio agreed to help and proposed that we take a trip to Virginia. His older brother knew of a place where I could potentially acquire a fake social security number. While the idea seemed morally wrong and illegal, desperation clouded my judgment, and I entertained the idea as a means to an end.

Arriving at the destination, I noticed a rundown building on a quiet street. The air felt heavy with uncertainty, and it seemed like time stood still. We entered the establishment cautiously, greeted by a tired-looking man who seemed to know Antonio's brother.

The atmosphere inside was dimly lit, with a musty scent that lingered in the air. As we exchanged words with the man behind the counter, my heart raced with anticipation. He presented us with a series of paperwork outlining the process and the necessary payment. It was a surreal moment as I scanned the forms, fully aware of the risks and consequences that were hidden behind the decision I was about to make. With shaky hands, I signed the documents, my mind filled with anxiety and determination.

The man processed our paperwork swiftly, his face expressionless as he handed me a fake social security number. Walking out of the building, I couldn't help but feel a whirlwind of conflicting emotions. Relief mingled with a lingering sense of guilt and unease.

I knew what we had just done was not the right way to handle my legal status, yet I had allowed desperation to guide my actions. At that time, the fear was overwhelming. I felt stuck, and uncertainty clouded my mind. In April 2001, Antonio and I decided to keep things simple and married at Newburgh City Hall. The ceremony was just us, two witnesses, and some papers, but it meant a lot to us, even without all the fancy stuff. After tying the knot, I landed a job at a dollar store near Antonio's parents' place. It was like a breath of fresh air to have a job again and not rely solely on Antonio's support. Don't get me wrong; I was grateful for his help over the past year, but there's just something about standing on your own two feet.

Working at the dollar store became my daily routine. It wasn't the flashiest job, but it gave me a sense of purpose. Chatting with customers and handling my tasks felt like I was part of something. The job might not have been glamorous, but it was mine, and that made all the difference.

Coming home after a shift, there was this warm feeling of satisfaction. I didn't need to depend solely on Antonio for money, and that was a game-changer. The dollar store gig might have been small, but it symbolized my journey to rebuild and take charge of my life.

In the grand scheme of things, that job at the dollar store was a big deal for me. It meant independence, stability, and a fresh start. It might not have been the fanciest job in town, but it was mine and brought back a sense of purpose and control.

As the weeks passed without any movement toward filing for residency, a sense of unease settled within me. I couldn't shake the feeling that Antonio wasn't inclined to sponsor my legal status, leaving me in a state of uncertainty. The absence of visits to an immigration lawyer intensified this growing concern. During this period, an "aha moment" struck me like a lightning bolt. It became apparent that Antonio's reluctance to assist with my legal status was more than just a delay – it was a method of control. It hit me that he was wielding this situation as a means to have power over me. The realization came to me like a quiet storm, revealing a facet of our relationship I hadn't fully grasped before.

In my reflection, I noticed Antonio's lack of initiative to support my immigration process. The weight of understanding that I might not receive help for an extended period sank in. It became evident that his support was contingent on his desire for control.

As this realization settled, I found myself questioning our relationship dynamics. I began to understand that Antonio's hesitance to assist with legal status wasn't just about bureaucracy; it was a deliberate choice to maintain dominance. Soon, I fully understood that the need for control clouded Antonio's intentions. It was as if he held the key to my future, dangling it just out of reach. The power dynamic became palpable, and a surge of emotions, ranging from frustration to resignation, coursed through me.

In a moment of self-discovery, I acknowledged the strength within me. Antonio, sensing this awakening, grew apprehensive. He understood that I still possessed the resilience to break free, to utter a firm "enough," and to walk away.

It was a turning point, a realization that I deserved more than a relationship built on control and power. The courage to stand up for myself, fueled by a newfound awareness, became the catalyst for a journey toward independence and a life where I dictated my own path. The next morning dawned with a newfound clarity. As I opened my eyes, a resolute power filled my being – today was the day I would break free from Antonio's control.

"Today is the day I leave him," I told myself repeatedly.

And to my surprise, there was no dramatic argument or heated exchange; instead, a quiet resolve settled within me. Taking a deep breath, I turned to Antonio and calmly uttered the words that had been echoing in my mind, "I'm leaving you, and I'm taking my son." His initial reaction was unexpected – a laugh that carried a hint of disbelief. "Ok, Maria. Good luck!" he responded casually, as if my decision was inconsequential.

The atmosphere in the apartment was charged with unspoken tension as I made my announcement. Antonio's laughter was unexpected, making a weird contrast to the serious talk. It seemed like he didn't really get how big a deal it was, or maybe he thought it was just a temporary frustration.

I took a deep breath, understanding it was more than just leaving physically; it was about finding myself again and putting my and my son's well-being first. Even though the road ahead was uncertain, the certainty of needing to break free from a harmful situation pushed me forward.

Leaving meant facing the challenges of starting over – finding a place to stay, getting a stable job, and rebuilding not only my life but also my son's. Despite the added complexity of being undocumented, I was fully prepared to take on the risk, as staying in an abusive relationship was no longer an option for me. That moment marked the beginning of my journey toward independence.

The laughter that first met my decision faded away, replaced by the realization that I was taking control of my own life. As the truth of leaving sank in, I felt empowered. Walking away from a controlling relationship wasn't just about protecting myself; it was a statement of my independence. Antonio's laid-back response strengthened my determination as I stepped into a life where my choices were truly mine.

Closing the door behind me, the weight of the decision pressed on my chest as I packed essentials for myself and my son. It was a challenging start, but I knew it was the right path for a brighter future.

Each item carefully placed in a bag carried the weight of my determination to forge a different path, one free from the control and uncertainty that defined my relationship with Antonio.

Without wasting a moment, I reached out to my cousin Lena in Plattekill, NY, sharing my decision and asking for her support. The morning was consumed with packing, carefully gathering my and my son's belongings.

As the afternoon sun painted the sky, Lena arrived to pick us up. The sight of her familiar face brought a wave of comfort, a reassurance that I wasn't alone in this endeavor. Loading our packed lives into her car, there was an unspoken understanding between us – this was a journey toward a new beginning, a chance to break free from the constraints of a stifling situation. I knew full well that the road ahead was uncertain, but the sense of liberation overshadowed any apprehension. At that moment of departure, I had no concrete plans or a detailed roadmap for the future. But what I did have was faith — a deep-seated belief that everything would work out for the best. It was a leap of faith into the unknown, guided by the conviction that I deserved more and the strength to embrace the uncertainty.

The unfamiliarity of my surroundings paled compared to the newfound freedom that enveloped me. I had taken the first steps toward a life where I dictated my own story, unburdened by the controlling forces of the past. I had tons of thoughts running through my mind. But everything was blurred in front of the feeling of departure from a past that no longer defined me.

The fear was growing in my heart that I would be navigating the challenges of starting over in the coming days and weeks. But in that moment, the simple act of walking away was a triumph— a declaration of resilience and self-worth that would set the tone for the chapters yet to be written.

Chapter 11: The Unbearable

In the poorly lit kitchen, I found myself sitting on the cold floor, curled up in a ball. The world felt heavy, and with every breath, I just wanted a way out, a break from all this pressure. I had a half bottle of 1 mg hydromorphone pills in my shaky hand, tempting me with the idea of comfort. Next to it, the Tylenol and ibuprofen bottles were there, seeming like a desperate option in my pained mind.

A battle raged inside me, a tough argument between giving up and pushing through. The kitchen's quietness made my thoughts of despair louder. The pain I felt wasn't only physical; it was attacking my soul non-stop. It cut through me like a sharp knife, as if someone was tormenting me relentlessly.

The debate in my mind intensified, a tumultuous back-and-forth between the longing for relief and the fear of the unknown. Each pill held the promise of a temporary reprieve, but at what cost? The room was silent, save for the haunting whispers of self-doubt, amplifying the profound loneliness that engulfed me.

Tears rolled down my face, mixing with the intense numbness all around me. I couldn't take my eyes off the pills; they seemed both tempting and terrifying. With every passing second, my agony got worse, like the world was slowly crushing me.

In this emotional tempest, the pain coursed through me. It was not just physical but a raw, visceral ache that resonated with the echoes of past wounds. It was as if the universe conspired to make every heartbeat a reminder of the stabbing sorrow etched into my soul. My trembling hands reached for the bottles, fingers dancing on the precipice of a fateful decision. The air was thick with the scent of despair, the taste of uncertainty lingering on my tongue.

I wished for relief, a way out of this internal chaos. But there, in that lonely kitchen, I knew the choice I was thinking about was dangerous. Taking those pills meant giving in to the darkness, surrendering to a place I might not come back from.

I had been knocked out by sleep for most of the morning, my body drained from all the tears that had taken over me the night before. The non-stop crying, the feeling of despair, and that hollow emptiness refused to let up. As I sat there, I shifted my eyes to the bottles beside me, wondering if I should just end the pain once and for all. But then, something deep inside me woke up, making me stop dead in my tracks. Was it my strong spirit, saying no way was this the end? Or maybe it was the thought of my kids, the amazing love they unknowingly showered on me, pulling me away from the brink of darkness.

Every time I got those thoughts about ending it, the faces of my kids flashed in my mind like a lifeline, snapping me back to reality. They were my saviors, the reason I clung on when everything looked dark. The clock on the wall reminded me it was almost 2:45, just fifteen minutes before my daughter's school day wrapped up. As I weighed the consequences of what I was thinking and the impact it'd have on those innocent souls depending on me, the decision became crystal clear. At that moment, I just couldn't do it. I couldn't bring myself to take those pills.

The room felt heavy with the weight of my struggle. A silent scream echoed within me as I battled with the darkness that threatened to consume my thoughts. The air was thick with desperation and a faint glimmer of hope, as if these emotions were engaged in a fierce tug-of-war for control over my weary soul.

The bottles, once temptations, now seemed like symbols of a crossroads in my life. I traced my finger over them, feeling the cold plastic and the gravity of my choices. The tears, held back for a moment, now streamed down my face like a river breaking through a dam. Each drop carried the weight of my pain, a pain that had become almost tangible in that dimly lit room.

In those agonizing minutes, I experienced a profound clash of emotions. The love for my children waged war against the unbearable pain within me. It was a battlefield where the battlefield itself was my own existence. The clock's ticking became a cruel reminder of time slipping away, yet it also held a promise of a future that could be salvaged.

With a trembling hand, I pushed the bottles away as an act of resistance against the pull of despair. The warmth of my tears mixed with the cold reality of the floor beneath me.

It has been almost two decades since I parted ways with Antonio, and let me tell you, those years were anything but a smooth ride. Trials and tribulations came knocking, pushing me to the edge and leaving me at rock bottom. Some mornings, the sheer heaviness of it all made dragging myself out of bed feel like an impossible feat. Yet, somehow, I mustered the strength to get up. There were responsibilities, a family relying on me, and work demanding my attention. But as time rolled on, the battles inside my head got fiercer. What started as occasional whispers of ending it all turned into a daily haunting, casting a shadow over every moment I was awake. It wasn't just some abstract idea anymore; it became a dark, heavy reality that clung to me, infiltrating my thoughts and emotions.

Every day felt like I was in a war zone within myself, desperately trying to clear through the depths of my despair. The plan to escape it all began taking shape in my mind, turning into a bone-chilling routine. It was as if I was crumbling under the weight of my own existence.

Emotions overwhelmed me – sadness, desperation, and feeling trapped. It was like fighting against a powerful tide, dragging me deeper into despair every day. Brief moments of relief were drowned out by persistent dark thoughts.

I craved a break, a chance to breathe without the weight on my shoulders. Even in those rare moments, the heaviness stuck around, making my life feel more like a storm than a calm journey. The tears held back for too long and flowed freely, merging with the invisible storm inside me. And in that storm, I questioned if there was a way out, if there was a chance for the sun to break through the dark clouds that hung over my existence.

In the middle of the night, the weight of my thoughts became suffocating. Working as a nurse in the Downtown Eastside of Vancouver, surrounded by the shadows of struggle, it felt like the darkness was creeping into my own soul. Fentanyl, a cruel temptation, lurked in the streets – a shortcut to end it all without enduring more pain. The idea haunted me relentlessly, a daily companion in my thoughts. Each day seemed like a monotonous loop, filled with the heavy burden of pain I had carried throughout my entire life. As a nurse, I knew too well the pathways to find that escape. It was like standing on the edge, a dangerous waltz with the idea of a painless exit. I found myself contemplating it over and over, a constant replay in the backdrop of my mind.

The desire to leave this earth in a painless way became my silent plea. Pain had been my lifelong companion, an unwelcome guest that overstayed its welcome. It was as if I had worn the cloak of suffering for so long that it had become a part of me. The monotony of pain had worn me down, and I reached a point where I just couldn't bear it anymore.

In those moments of deep contemplation, I yearned for relief, a respite from the ceaseless ache. The longing for peace was etched in every sigh, every gaze cast into the abyss of my own thoughts. It wasn't a cry for attention but a desperate plea for an end to the pain that had defined my existence.

Yet, even in the darkest corners of my mind, a flicker of something held me back. Was it fear, a glimmer of hope, or the lingering connection to a life I hadn't fully explored? The emotions tangled within me – a complex web of despair, longing, and a desperate search for a way out of this relentless cycle.

In the core of my being, a silent struggle was going on. Despite the dark thoughts and the constant pull toward an escape, there was a stubborn part of me that clung to life. It yearned to keep fighting, to endure, to find a way to keep living.

In the chaos of my emotions, a small flicker of hope whispered that maybe, just maybe, things could turn around for me. As a nurse in the heart of Downtown Eastside, where the streets echoed with pain, it was tempting to reach for that quick exit in the form of fentanyl. Yet, I held back. I never asked my clients for that deadly substance, knowing deep down that I needed to resist the lure of a painless end. The battle within me persisted, a daily struggle against the shadows that threatened to consume my spirit.

The thoughts of suicide were a relentless storm, thundering in the background of my mind. I found myself standing on the edge, pills in hand, the temptation to swallow them hanging heavy in the air. It was like a struggle with the abyss – moments when I brought the pills close to my mouth, feeling the weight of the decision I was teetering on. But, somehow, I never let them pass my lips.

Each time the pills hovered near, it was a confrontation with the darkness, a confrontation with myself. In those moments, I grappled with the contradiction of wanting to live yet being overwhelmed by the desire to escape the pain. The pills were a choice I hadn't fully made – a line I hesitated to cross. It was as if I was standing at the crossroads of existence, torn between the pull of despair and the faint glimmer of resilience within. The unspoken plea for a lifeline echoed through the quiet moments, a plea for a reason to keep holding on.

Mike, my partner, became the unfortunate witness to the battles within my mind. It was he who stumbled upon me, defeated, with a bottle in my hand. Over time, the toll on his own mental health was becoming evident. The burden of seeing me making a complete mess was taking a toll on him. He was the one who had to pick me up from the lowest points, heartbroken and shattered.

In his face, I saw a reflection of the pain that mirrored my own. The desperation and disappointment carved on his features were like silent screams, telling the tale of a struggle he couldn't fully comprehend. His eyes, once filled with warmth, now carried the weight of witnessing someone he loved slipping away into the void of their own thoughts.

The heaviness in our shared silence spoke volumes. I could feel the weight of his concern, his love, and the overwhelming frustration of not being able to fix the broken pieces of me. Mike became a silent hero in my life, catching me every time I fell, but I could sense the impact it had on him. The weariness in his eyes mirrored the fatigue of trying to save someone who felt beyond saving.

This wasn't just my battle; it was ours. Mike's silent support held me together at times, but I could see the cracks forming in his own resilience. The cycle of witnessing my struggle, picking up the shattered pieces, and feeling the sting of disappointment became the rhythm of our shared existence.

Those few years felt like an endless rollercoaster of highs and lows. Some days, I could put on a brave face, hiding the turmoil within. I became a master of pretending, especially at work, wearing a mask that shielded the truth. Nobody outside the walls of my home knew the depth of the struggle. Constant sadness, fatigue, and anger became like old friends, unwelcome but always present. They seeped into my identity, shaping who I was and overshadowing any glimpse of joy. I became skilled at the art of asking our creator what I did to deserve this relentless pain and suffering. It was a plea to make sense of the chaos that seemed to cling to me like an unwanted companion following my every step.

The weight of despair felt like a heavy cloak, dragging me down wherever I went. Catching my breath became a rare luxury, and I found myself wondering if peace would forever elude me. The pain was so palpable that recalling those times now brings it rushing back. It's like reopening old wounds that never fully healed.

In those moments, I longed for my higher self – a version of me untouched by past scars. Rising above this pain felt like an uphill battle, each step a struggle against haunting memories. I wanted to break free from the past's chains, to breathe without that heavy burden.

I felt nostalgia for the person I used to be and a burning determination to become someone stronger. It's a battle between the echoes of pain and the whispered promises of a better future. In acknowledging the pain, there's a recognition that healing is a process, and the journey toward the higher self is a step-by-step ascent from the depths of despair.

A Message from My Higher Self:

Maria, you've been through a lot. You've hit rock bottom more times than you can count, and each time, you've managed to rise above it all. It's truly amazing to see how far you've come. You've developed some incredible tools and coping mechanisms along the way, which show just how strong and resilient you are. Even in your darkest moments, your faith has guided you and propelled you forward. It's been a guiding light, giving you the strength to keep going.

When you look back on your journey, it's clear that things have aligned in your favor. It's a testament to the power of acknowledging and releasing your emotions. It's like magic - the way your pain and wounds have transformed into wisdom. It's a powerful achievement.

You've realized that you don't need someone else to save you. You are your own hero. You've freed yourself from the control and manipulation that exists in the world. Your healing and self-discovery have become your mission, awakening the hero within you. It's a transformational journey filled with resilience, wisdom, and incredible inner strength.

You should be proud of yourself, Maria. Your ability to overcome adversity and turn pain into power is truly inspiring. Keep embracing your strength, and keep moving forward on your journey. You're capable of achieving anything.

Chapter 12: The Healing Journey

"The real difficulty is to overcome how you think of yourself."

- Maya Angelou

I've sat in many therapist offices, opening up about my deepest feelings and recounting the traumas of my childhood. It's been an emotional rollercoaster, to say the least. There have been times when I left those sessions feeling completely hopeless, even worse than when I walked in. It can be incredibly frustrating, especially when you've been searching for the right therapist for what feels like an eternity. But trust me, when you find the person who truly understands and provides the support you need, hold onto them tightly.

It's like finding a lifeline in the vast ocean of emotions. When you finally connect with a therapist who gets you, it's like a weight has been lifted off your shoulders. They help you navigate through the labyrinth of your emotions, providing a safe space for you to explore your innermost thoughts. Their ability to empathize with your struggles, to truly understand the pain you've endured, is like a soothing balm to your wounded soul.

In their presence, you are free to let your emotions flow and to express yourself without fear of judgment. They listen attentively, their eyes filled with compassion, as you pour out your heart. Every word you utter, every tear you shed, is met with understanding and validation. They have this incredible knack for putting your feelings into words when you can't find them yourself, like a skilled translator bridging the gap between your inner turmoil and the outside world. But it's not just their words that offer solace; it's the way they make you feel seen and heard. It's in the gentle touch of their hand when you're overwhelmed with grief or the encouraging smile they give when you manage to take a small step forward. They create a safe haven where you can find comfort and healing, where your emotions are not dismissed or belittled.

Finding the right therapist is like finding a rare gem in a vast desert. So, when you stumble upon that gem, don't let go. Cherish their presence in your life because, in a world that can sometimes feel cold and indifferent, they offer warmth and understanding. Seek solace in their guidance, knowing that they are there to support you through the ups and downs of your healing journey.

In the end, it's not just their professional expertise that matters but the genuine human connection they foster. Keep them close, for they hold the key to unlocking the strength within you. They are the catalysts for transformation, guiding you toward a future filled with hope and healing.

Well, the healing journey is all about exploring the right path for your life. It's like choosing the right plotline and screenplay for your story, where you are the director of your life, picking scenes and frames that are better suited for the story of your life.

After much consideration, I made the decision to try antidepressants. At first, they provided some stability to my mood, but I didn't experience much joy in life. However, the introduction of meditation in late 2021 marked a transformative turning point in my journey. Meditation emerged as a catalyst for my healing. It facilitated an inward focus, enabling a profound connection with emotions long suppressed within my body. This practice acted as a conduit, releasing a flood of emotions—anger, sadness, shame, guilt, and fear—rising to the surface of my conscious awareness.

Within the sacred meditation space, I granted myself the freedom to experience and process each emotion without judgment. Though challenging, confronting these intense emotions proved to be incredibly liberating.

Continuing the practice of meditation revealed the alchemical power within me. I learned to transmute these intense emotions into sources of empowerment, fueling my personal growth and resilience. Through meditation, I embraced the process of transforming pain and fear into wellsprings of strength.

As meditation became a daily practice, I discovered the ability to reconnect with and shift the energy within my body. The calmness and stillness within became a sanctuary, offering solace and facilitating healing. It evolved into a tool for processing emotions and finding inner peace amidst life's chaos.

In the ongoing healing journey, meditation emerged as the key to unlocking the door to my inner power. Each time I sat in stillness, breathing deeply and grounding myself, I could feel the emotional weight lifting and a sense of lightness washing over me.

For those seeking a transformative path on their healing journey, I recommend exploring the practice of meditation. It requires no specialized equipment or skills and can be as simple as finding a quiet space, closing one's eyes, and focusing on the breath. Grant yourself the gift of going inward, allowing hidden emotions to be acknowledged and ultimately transformed. Embrace the alchemical power within and let meditation be a guide on the path to healing and self-discovery.

Your inner turmoil serves as a beacon, urging you to delve deeper into your being and challenge your beliefs and self-perception. It's not an easy task to do as it precipitates an identity crisis. Nevertheless, this process is crucial as it exposes the illusions, belief systems, and dogmas upon which we've constructed our identities. Although daunting for the ego, embracing this journey allows you to perceive reality from your higher self and transcend thought. Eventually, you'll recognize that what you're undergoing is the genesis of a profound personal metamorphosis –an evolution toward empowerment, utter presence, and infinite awareness.

In the course of my meditation journey, I unearthed a deeper understanding of the core issues impacting my mental well-being. Recognizing the need for a proactive approach, I delved into the deepest parts of my being, aiming to reveal the root causes of my pain. This involved confronting aspects of myself that harbored fear, shame, guilt, and brokenness—like fragmented pieces yearning for acknowledgment and understanding.

I discovered that these neglected facets of my identity were desperately seeking visibility and resonance. Laden with emotional weight, craved validation. I made a deliberate choice to grant them my undivided attention and awareness. I started an inner journey, exploring the experiences and traumas that had fostered disconnection within myself.

Exploring the origins of my pain and disconnection proved to be a challenging undertaking, demanding courage, vulnerability, and a readiness to confront discomfort. By bringing these concealed aspects to light, I started unraveling layers of conditioning and societal expectations that contributed to my sense of disconnection.

With each stride toward self-awareness, I gradually re-established connections with suppressed or overlooked aspects of myself. Offering compassion and understanding, I embraced their presence rather than pushing them away. Through this process, I began weaving together the fractured pieces of myself, progressively reclaiming a sense of wholeness and healing. Discovering the root causes of my disconnection unveiled a path to a deeper self-reconnection. Embarking on this journey required self-reflection, introspection, and a willingness to confront personal pain. Yet, during this exploration, I commenced the mending of broken aspects and nurtured a growing sense of inner harmony.

If you're on a quest for healing, fear not the journey into the depths of your being. Take the time to explore the root of your pain and disconnection. Give neglected parts of yourself the attention and awareness they crave. Through this voyage of self-discovery, healing becomes possible as you reclaim your power and cultivate a stronger connection with your authentic self.

As I tenderly nurture those fractured pieces of myself, I embrace them with love and gratitude. I hold them close, understanding that they once guarded me in moments of ignorance. Through this act of acceptance, a profound sense of connectedness blossoms within my mind, body, and soul. While sitting in peaceful silence, I reflect on the thoughts woven into my being. I venture to question the very essence of my thoughts and the logic behind them.

Intense curiosity begins to stir, unraveling the intricate threads of my thinking process. It is here that I uncover the true nature of my thoughts – those very thoughts that influence my behavior, shape my reactions and manifest as my reality. In embracing this truth, a wealth of emotions, expressions, and sensations emerge, breathing life into the simple language that captures the essence of my transformation. In my ongoing healing journey, I've been embracing those wounded parts of myself with love. It's a process of accepting them and thanking them for doing their best to shield me when I wasn't fully aware. This practice has sparked a profound sense of connection with my mind, body, and soul.

Taking moments to sit quietly with me has become a sanctuary for reflection on my thought patterns. It's like having a conversation with the deepest layers of my being. I express gratitude to those protective parts of myself, acknowledging their efforts in times of unawareness.

This journey of self-love has opened up a channel of understanding between me and myself. It's like I've invited those neglected aspects to the table and offered them a seat of honor. Through this acceptance, the connection with my inner world has deepened, creating a harmonious alignment between my thoughts, emotions, and actions.

As I continue this practice, a sense of curiosity blossoms within me. I find myself questioning the nature of my thoughts and the patterns they weave. It's like peeling back the layers to uncover the driving force behind my behaviors, reactions, and, ultimately, the reality I create.

This exploration of thought and behavior isn't always easy. It requires patience and a gentle touch. Yet, in those quiet moments of self-reflection, I've unearthed a newfound awareness. It's as if I'm decoding the language of my own mind, deciphering the messages that guide my journey. The emotions that accompany this process are like a symphony—sometimes harmonious, sometimes discordant. There's a balance between gratitude for the lessons learned and the tenderness required to nurture those wounded parts. It's a journey filled with discovery, where each moment of introspection becomes a step toward personal transformation.

In the silence of self-reflection, I find a canvas to paint the picture of my reality. It's not about erasing the past but rather acknowledging it with compassion. By sitting quietly, I've become both the observer and the artist, crafting a narrative that aligns with the person I'm becoming. This journey of self-discovery is a masterpiece in the making, woven with threads of love, acceptance, and the gentle unraveling of old thought patterns.

As I delved deeper into my quest for a better quality of life, a realization struck me like a gentle whisper: to truly change my experiences, I had to start transforming from within. It's crystal clear that external factors and social stuff can impact our mental health. Yet, this is where the magic of healing steps in.

Healing, to me, is this beautiful journey of accepting and loving every single part of yourself. It's like gazing at a painting and recognizing the delicate artistry in your own life, acknowledging the hurdles you've conquered. It's about facing those challenges head-on and ditching the labels you or society slapped on you. Healing is reclaiming the confidence to tackle whatever life throws your way.

A big part of this journey is reconnecting with yourself—your body, mind, and soul. It's about realizing that the tough times weren't punishments but signals from your soul, shouting that you were disconnected. And here's the kicker: the power to find your way back home was always within you. This journey is not just a change in mindset; it's a whirlwind of emotions. There are moments of profound acceptance, where you hug your past self and say, "I get it now." It involves facing and overcoming obstacles, learning from them, and using them to build a better version of yourself.

Picture shedding the heavy labels like old clothes, making room for a wardrobe of self-love and acceptance. It's like finding a hidden treasure within yourself—gems of resilience, strength, and wisdom that were waiting to be discovered.

The experience of healing feels like rewiring your mindset. You take a step back, examine your thoughts, and toss out the ones that don't serve you. It's a bit like decluttering a messy room, creating space for positivity and growth.

As you embrace the challenges, there's a sense of liberation. It's like setting free caged birds within you—your aspirations, dreams, and the true essence of who you are. It's a process of untangling the knots, allowing your authentic self to shine.

In the quiet moments of self-reflection, there's a symphony of emotions—gratitude, acceptance, and a touch of vulnerability. It's not about erasing the past but reshaping it into a narrative that empowers you. This healing journey is like an adventure, with each step leading you back to the most important place—home, to yourself.

Since I'm reminiscing about my journey, let me take you back to a beautiful experience I had just a few months ago. Thanks to this incident, I was able to realize and accept a profound reality. It was one of those normal days when I was immersed in my usual meditation routine, and I found myself lost in the vast stream of universal consciousness. It was a realm where the boundaries of time and space blurred, and I felt a deep connection to the pulsating energy of the universe. In this profound state, my senses became heightened, and I beheld a mesmerizing symphony of colors and shapes orchestrated by the universe itself.

But then, out of nowhere, the scenery shifted. Suddenly, I found myself bombarded with images. I witnessed a series of scenes that left me breathless and heartbroken. In my vision, I saw countless individuals lying on the ground, their bodies motionless and unconscious. Overwhelmed by the intensity of the sight, I could sense their fragile hold on life, as if they were desperately clinging to a thread.

The emotions that swept over me in that moment were indescribable. It was like a tidal wave of concern, empathy, and a desire to understand the meaning behind these vivid visions. In the realm of meditation, where the boundaries of the physical world dissolve, I was confronted with a stark reality that begged for exploration and understanding.

In this surreal cinematic journey within my meditation, the scenes displayed like chapters of a story, each more gripping than the last. I found myself in the middle of a crisis, responding to overdoses alongside my colleagues. The collective urgency, the shared mission to save a life, pulsed through every frame.

As if the universe zoomed in, the focus narrowed down to a single individual. It was a peculiar sensation, akin to being both an observer and an active participant in this drama. The emotions surged, a rollercoaster of empathy, responsibility, and an overwhelming connection to the unfolding narrative. In this vivid sequence, I could see myself dialing 911, my fingers moving with urgency as the person lay on the ground, unconscious, and their breath held hostage by the grip of an overdose.

The 911 operator's voice cut through the chaos, asking those critical questions – "Is the person breathing? Are they conscious or unconscious?" It struck me deeply that in that crucial moment, the operator didn't inquire about the individual's appearance, gender, or ethnic background. The essence of the person lay in the simple truth – are they breathing, are they conscious?

And then, like a lightning bolt of realization, it hit me. The truth of who we are, a question that always lingers in our head to which we often seek answers, is actually right before our eyes. We are consciousness. We are souls. The distinctions that divide us in the waking world dissolve in the face of this universal truth. It was a revelation that transcended the boundaries of the ordinary, an understanding that we are, at our core, interconnected beings sharing the essence of consciousness.

In the crucible of a life-or-death scenario, the essence of our being is laid bare, stripped down to the core truth – consciousness. In that pivotal moment, nothing else holds weight.

Not your personality, physical appearance, emotions, or thoughts – all these layers peel away, revealing the raw truth. It's a profound unveiling, a stark realization that in the face of life's most critical junctures, the essence of who you are is consciousness. In that intense scene within the meditation, I grasped the fundamental truth that transcends the superficial aspects of our existence. The body, with all its intricacies, is merely a vessel – a means for us to navigate this physical world, to craft our experiences, lessons, and destiny. It struck me that your breath serves as the bridge connecting your body and mind. It is the life force that animates this vessel, linking the tangible and the intangible aspects of your being.

Feelings of awe, reverence, and a sense of connection accompanied this revelation. It was like witnessing the universal symphony, where the harmony of existence is conducted through the simple act of breathing. The understanding that deep down, we are conscious beings, and our breath connects all aspects of our human existence was like getting hands on a powerful armor in a battle.

Chapter 13: Everything Is Perspective

Unlocking the potential to shape your destiny involves breaking free from the patterns that define you and forging a new path. Dr. Joe Dispenza's words echo the profound truth that altering our outcomes necessitates the bold act of reinventing ourselves.

"If you want a new outcome, you will have to break the habit of being yourself and reinvent a new self."

- Dr. Joe Dispenza

Imagine a world where you hold the power to reprogram your brain and mold your subconscious mind. It's a place where you can dismantle the stronghold of negative, self-sabotaging thoughts and replace them with empowering ones that pave the way for a life brimming with limitless possibilities.

In recent times, I've found myself deeply engrossed in the fascinating exploration of how the simple yet effective practices of meditation and spirituality can cast a transformative spell on our mind, body, and soul.

It's like discovering a secret passage to reshape the very fabric of our existence. The journey isn't just about understanding this power; it's about feeling its impact on a visceral level. It's about transcending the limitations of habitual thinking and embracing the potential for radical change.

As I researched more about this practice, I found it to be an odyssey of self-discovery and empowerment. It's not merely about adopting a new mindset; it's about rewiring the very circuitry of our thoughts. The emotions that accompany this journey are like currents propelling us toward uncharted territories, stirring a sense of excitement, wonder, and, at times, a bit of trepidation.

According to Dr. Joe Dispenza, a well-known researcher, and author, a whopping 95% of who we are is shaped by programming. This programming isn't just a set of instructions; it molds our behaviors, habits, beliefs, attitudes, and even our emotional reactions. It's like an invisible force shaping the lens through which we see the world. All of this is tucked away in the corners of our subconscious.

Let me shed light on something intriguing. If you've been through some tough times or trauma, you might find yourself strangely cozy with negative emotions. It's like they become your daily companions – sadness, anger, anxiety – they settle in, making themselves right at home.

Dr. Joe points out that people in this situation tend to cling to these emotions, and they even need external conditions to validate and keep their addiction alive. It's like your problems, financial struggles, or fears become the supporting cast in the drama of your emotional life.

Dr. Dispenza talks about emotional addictions. He says that it's like living in a loop, the kind that messes with how you see the world around you. It's like wearing glasses that tint everything with the shades of your survival emotions. And guess what? This distorted view becomes a self-fulfilling prophecy, a cycle that keeps churning.

Now, let's talk about stress chemicals. Dr. Joe says that being stuck in survival mode for too long makes you a bit too friendly with stress chemicals. It's like your body gets hooked on them, and breaking free seems almost impossible. The longer we stay in this survival mode, the more we get hooked on stress chemicals. Dr. Dispenza suggests a way out of this dilemma, elevating your thoughts above your current feelings. This is a game-changer. He believes swapping negative thoughts to uplifting ones can disrupt the whole cycle.

It's like hitting the reset button on your mind, breaking free from the chains of your past. He has briefly described this phenomenon in his book *"Becoming Supernatural: How Common People are Doing the Uncommon."* The words in there echo the idea that changing your thoughts can be the key to liberating yourself from the grip of those once-commanding negative thoughts and emotions.

In addition to this, let's take a dig at Dr. Joe Dispenza's insights about meditation – it's like a backstage pass to your inner world. According to him, meditation isn't just about sitting cross-legged and chanting; it's a journey within. As you meditate, you get to know your thoughts, your emotions, and your behaviors. It's like turning on the lights in the room you've been avoiding.

Dr. Joe explains that meditation becomes a superhero tool, swooping in to rescue you from the cycle of negative thoughts and emotions. It's like a power-up that grants you the strength to conquer yourself.

And you know what? I've been down that road. Personally, diving into meditation boosted my awareness levels. Suddenly, I had this grip over thoughts that used to pull me in all directions.

And if you ask about the result. Well, I became the architect of my own reality. My thoughts and emotions weren't just passengers anymore; they were my co-pilots, steering me toward a new perspective. It's like I upgraded my mental software, and the reality I started to build reflected this fresh outlook. All thanks to the transformative magic of meditation, just as Dr. Joe Dispenza beautifully puts it in "Becoming Supernatural: How Common People are Doing the Uncommon."

"As you take your attention off your past-present reality or your predictable future reality, you are calling energy back to you and building your own electromagnetic field. Now, you have the energy to heal yourself or create a new experience in your life. Not surprisingly, your attention eventually begins to wander again."

Now, let's talk about how we can pull off this incredible transformation. Dr. Dispenza brings in some brainy science to the rescue. According to neuroscience, dedicating just one hour a day to a single concept, a solitary idea, can work wonders. It's like giving your brain a power workout – potentially doubling the number of connections in there.

This whole magic trick is called neuroplasticity. In simple terms, it means that when you focus on something new, your brain makes new connections. It's like upgrading your mental software once again. These new connections don't just chill in your brain space; they lead to new behaviors. It's like rewiring your brain for a better version of you. And these changes aren't just happening in your thoughts. They're causing ripples in your biology. Dr. Joe explains it like this:

"The brain is organized to reflect everything we know in our environment. And for the most part, our brain is equal to our

environment."

In other words, changing what's going on in your head isn't just a mental shift – it's like remodeling the very structure of your brain. So, that hour of focused thinking each day is like your brain's daily workout for a healthier, happier you. Science meets self-improvement – and it's pretty amazing.

"When you change, everything changes around you."

— Joe Dispenza, Rewired, Dr. Joe Dispenza, Unlimited

Delving Into the Intersection of Mental Health and Spirituality:

"The Western culture has consistently ignored the birth of the healer."

- Dr. Somé

Now, let's dive into the wisdom of Dr. Malidoma Somé, a wise elder from West Africa's Dagara tribe. This man was no ordinary sage – he held not one, not two, but three Master's degrees and two Doctorates. He was a real brainiac, but his brilliance didn't just shine in academics; he was a great spiritual leader, recognized for his deep understanding of rituals, community, and healing.

Dr. Some had a unique take on mental illness. He didn't see it as a curse but rather as the birth of a new healer. That's a radical shift from the way the West often views mental health. When he set foot in the United States in the 1980s, he was pretty shocked at how people here dealt with mental illness. His belief was pretty out there – he saw people grappling with mental challenges as chosen vessels. They were, according to him, messengers from the spirit realm, here to communicate vital messages to the community. Dr. Some boldly stated that mental illnesses should be seen as spiritual distress. It's like a call for a healer to step into the spotlight.

According to him, every human being, no matter where they're from, yearns for two things: the full realization of their innate gifts and the approval, acknowledgment, and confirmation of these gifts. It's like he's saying we're all in this together, seeking our purpose and wanting our unique talents to be seen and celebrated.

Well, we can't deny the unfortunate truth that Dr. Malidoma identified in society. See, he believed that the West has a bit of a blind spot when it comes to recognizing and nurturing these incredible gifts.

"There is an inner power and authority that fails to shine because the world around them is blind to it."

— Malidoma Patrice Somé,

The Healing Wisdom of Africa: Finding Life Purpose Through Nature, Ritual, and Community

In his eyes, the Western approach to mental health, with its heavy reliance on a medical model, doesn't quite hit the mark. Dr. Some argued that many individuals with unique talents and inner power find themselves in a tough spot. Why?

Because the world around them is, as he put it, "blind to it." It's like having a powerful light within, but the world outside doesn't have the right lenses to see its brilliance. Dr. Some had a knack for articulating profound thoughts, and he didn't hold back in sharing his wisdom. Unfortunately, he passed away in 2021, but his legacy lives on through messages like these – powerful reminders that there's more to mental health than meets the eye.

"It is possible that we have been brought together at this time because we have profound truths to teach each other. Toward that end, I offer the wisdom of the African ancestors so that Westerners might find the deep healing they seek. The spark of this ancestral flame, which I have brought to the stranger's land, is now burning brightly. Increasingly, I have been and will be encouraging Westerners to embody these traditions as a testimony to the indigenous capacity to assert itself with dignity in the face of modernity. In this way, the ancestors will know that this medicine has found a true home- that it is more than an honored guest. At this critical time in history, the earth's people are awakening to a deep need for global healing. African wisdom, so long held secret, is being called on to provide tools to enable us to move into a more peaceful and empowered way of being, both within ourselves and within our communities. The indigenous spirit in each of us is calling for cleansing and reconciliation. The ancestors are responding".

– Malidoma Some, The Healing Wisdom of Africa

During my spiritual awakening, I stumbled upon incredible gifts hidden within me. One such gift unveiled itself – the ability to receive messages through visions during meditation.

"That which we do not bring to consciousness appears in our life as fate."

— Carl Jung

I also came to know the power of a very common and underrated phenomenon – breathing. Breathing, the simple act that sustains life, is also the anchor to consciousness and presence. It's the very essence of our existence. To put this in perspective – when you're fully conscious of your truth, you're tuned into your surroundings, your thoughts, your emotions, your beauty, and everything that encompasses your being.

It's a state of awareness that empowers you, giving you control over your responses and reactions to life. Conversely, when you're unconscious, you navigate through existence in a vulnerable state. Unaware of your truth, you become a passenger rather than the driver of your life.

Your thoughts, behaviors, and emotions operate in the shadows, influencing your experiences without your conscious consent. Triggers go unnoticed, and you react rather than respond, perpetuating a cycle of suffering.

At the outset of "Opening Pandora's Box," Dr. Dispenza has revealed his discoveries regarding these visions. He noted that in the course of his research, he observed a growing number of individuals experiencing peculiar dreams and visions.

He explained that as we devote more time to being in beta waves, our dreams and visions will progress, becoming increasingly lucid. That is because the neurochemistry generated by our brains enables us to encounter more lucid moments, gaining consciousness within our subconscious mind.

"The only way to encounter the mystical is through the realm of unlimited universes that exist beyond the limited world of our senses. The mystical, then, is the unknown."[1]

- Feeling our way into the Mystical-

part 1 Dr. Joe Dispenza

Reflecting on my vision, I saw the stark contrast between living consciously and unconsciously. In that moment of vulnerability, the person in distress relied on others for salvation. Their fate hung in the balance, dictated by external actions rather than a deliberate path of destiny. This vision is a metaphor symbolizing the pervasive state of unconscious living dictated by our conditioning. We've overdosed on divisive propaganda, consumerism, dogmas, and social norms imposed by the system and those in power, shaping our thoughts, emotions, and behavior. This deliberate manipulation serves to keep us distracted and alienated from both ourselves and each other. However, it also instilled a sense of empowerment by highlighting our capacity to forge a new path and architect our destinies.

Feelings of empowerment, determination, and a fervent desire for self-directed destiny accompanied this revelation. It emphasized the importance of embracing consciousness, of being the conscious creator rather than an unwitting passenger in the journey of life. The choice to be aware, to breathe in the

____

[1] https://drjoedispenza.com/dr-joes-blog/feeling-our-way-into-the-mystical-part-i

essence of consciousness, became not just a revelation but a guiding principle for crafting one's destiny.

Enduring the weight of your emotions won't be fatal. Your body is equipped to manage and navigate through those complex feelings. Yet, suppressing them and attempting to evade them could prove detrimental. Hence, it is crucial to acknowledge your pain and your feelings but don't become the emotions. You can discern the roots of your emotions and reactions by delving into your patterns, behaviors, and triggers. Self-awareness serves as a compass, steering you toward the embodiment of the person you aspire to be and have the potential to become.

From the moment we are born, we are taught to perceive a division between our inner and outer realities. However, the truth is they are inherently unified. This perceived separation is merely an illusion perpetuated by our ego. Consequently, we fixate on external pursuits, seeking validation and material possessions. Driven by a longing for acceptance and fear of rejection, we conform to societal norms, inadvertently sacrificing our uniqueness, talents, and higher purpose. Consequently, we become detached from our authentic selves. However, once we understand that our outer experiences mirror our inner thoughts and emotions, we gain the power to reshape our experiences and manifest the life we yearn for.

Upon awakening, your perspective of reality will shift dramatically. Once you align with the flow of universal frequency, your entire perception of reality will undergo a profound transformation. Once you begin to connect with the universal consciousness, you will begin to gain insight into the fabric and true nature of reality. The veils of illusion will dissipate. Your awareness will transcend the confines of the material world, enabling profound understanding of both yourself and the world. At the same time, you come to understand that in this physical world there aren't inherently good or bad people; rather, there are those who are conscious and those who are unconscious. This shift moves you from judgment to comprehension. We often presume that others perceive the world through the same lens as us. However, in this material world, reality is far more complex. Each individual possesses a distinct and personal perspective of reality, influenced by their unique experiences and level of awareness. Recognizing the diversity of perspectives promotes understanding and acceptance.

How do you distinguish between someone who is conscious and someone who is merely acting out of habit or conditioning? It's their light. It's in the way they shine. A conscious individual exudes a different energy, marked by intention, purpose, and love. They embrace their authenticity despite imperfections and are committed to learning and evolving. They fearlessly confront challenges, always seeking self-improvement and driven by a desire to contribute to the greater good because they understand the interconnectedness of everything. They alchemize their inner struggles, transforming them into strengths.

Additionally, they emanate a radiant aura of self-love and compassion for all beings. They grasp the intricate balance between light and darkness, recognizing them as complementary forces akin to the yin and yang. They comprehend the inherent harmony in the universe, where everything, including ourselves, is composed of myriad atoms, each reliant on both negative and positive charges. Why would life be any different? You are life itself, inseparable from its entirety. You embody the spectrum of existence; darkness and light, feminine and masculine, positive and negative. You are the vast oceans, the towering mountains, the boundless sky, encompassing both your heaven and your hell.

Throughout my life journey, I have been filled with gratitude for every aspect of it. From the people I've encountered, both the good and the bad, to the challenges I've faced and the transformations I've undergone, I have learned valuable lessons from each and every soul who has crossed my path. I honor them all for their role in shaping my growth, even if it wasn't always easy. I am grateful for the difficult lessons that have come my way and for the emotions that have emerged as a result. Even the pain and sorrows have played a significant role in my life, for they have helped me appreciate the beauty and joy that exists. It is through experiencing a range of emotions, both positive and negative that I have come to truly understand the richness and complexity of life.

Although uncertain about what lies ahead for the rest of my life, I embrace everything I am meant to experience. My main intention is to live authentically, to be true to who I am at the core of my being. I desire to immerse myself in all that life fully has to offer – the highs and lows, the joys and sorrows. Above all, I want to cultivate the practice of dwelling in the present moment, for it is in the here and now that true living occurs.

Through the journey of self-discovery, I have reconnected with a precious part of myself that I hold dear and am determined to nurture.

The healing journey led me to this realization: Generational trauma and pain persist within a family lineage until someone is prepared to acknowledge, address, and let go of it. We've been conditioned to evade and normalize toxic behaviors instead of how to feel and regulate our emotions. However, you cannot heal what you're not capable of feeling. During my childhood, my developing mind was influenced by both my family and environment. Their thoughts, beliefs, and actions were molded by their own experiences and traumas, perpetuating a cycle of pain and suffering——a generational curse. Consequently, I inherited their pain and trauma, leading to cultivating a negative self-perception within me. As a result, I began to manifest precisely what I was thinking and feeling about myself, drawing in experiences that mirrored my feelings of unworthiness. Recognizing that I had shaped my reality based on my beliefs and internal emotions was a difficult truth to accept. Hence, breaking free from the cycle of generational trauma becomes imperative.

Simultaneously, this insight enlightened me to the incredible power we possess as human beings—the power of manifestation. Unfortunately, we are not educated about the potency of manifestation- the way our thoughts and emotions materialize in our external reality. It's akin to understanding the principle of cause and effect. To manifest the reality you genuinely crave, it's essential to revisit and heal the wounds of your inner child, which are hindering your progress. This involves reprogramming your subconscious mind to forge a new outcome in the present. By offering the love and safety your inner child lacked in the past, you can create a nurturing environment in the present moment. In other words, becoming conscious of your subconscious mind.

As we open our hearts and align with the rhythm of life, we find ourselves in harmony with the universe. It is in this state that a powerful transformation occurs, allowing us to shape our reality with love and authenticity. We come to realize that we are not mere spectators but active co-creators, holding the key to manifesting our own destinies.

Taking the path of self-discovery uncovers the truth of our authentic selves. It can be a bit daunting, but we shouldn't fear cracking open. In fact, through this process, we find rebirth and rediscover the radiant divine light that has always existed within us. This light, which may have been hidden or forgotten, is meant to shine through and guide us toward our true purpose. If we can face our fears and embrace vulnerability, we will discover that cracking open is not the end but the beginning of a profound transformation. We shed old layers and beliefs that no longer serve us, allowing our true essence to emerge. So, don't be afraid to crack open because, in doing so, we give ourselves the opportunity to be reborn and live in alignment with our authentic selves.